The Perfect Parent

Guiding Principles
from the Father-Heart of God

Dr. Doug Ley

The Perfect Parent: Guiding Principles from the Father-Heart of God

First Paperback Edition

Copyright © 2020 Serving Beyond Borders

Unless otherwise noted, Scripture quotations are taken from the New American Standard Bible (NASB), Copyright © 1960, 1962, 1963, 1968, 1971, 1972, 1973, 1975, 1995 by The Lockman Foundation. Used by permission. www.Lockman.org

Although every precaution has been taken to verify the accuracy of the information contained in this book, the author and publisher assume no responsibility for any errors or omissions. The information contained in this book is not intended to replace the professional opinion of a physician or health care professional. Consult your physician or health care professional prior to attempting to implement any of the suggestions or recommendations provided in this book. No liability is assumed for damages that may result from the use of information contained within.

Editorial project management: Corey McCullough, www.cbmcediting.com

Printed in the United States of America

ISBN: 978-1-7353015-0-1

Published by Serving Beyond Borders

10 9 8 7 6 5 4 3 2 1

Table of Contents

Dedication

To the One who rescued my soul from the pit of hell and pointed me to The Perfect Parent who loves me. And then You gave me the gift of a wife who loves You more than me. And then You blessed us with four children and called them each to follow You. And now our grandchildren.... You have done immeasurably more than I could ever imagine (and you know I have a wild imagination!). So, to You, Jesus I dedicate this work. To You be the glory, and honor, and power forever and ever and ever. Amen!

Introduction:
Parenting: Where is the Instruction Manual?

Everybody knows how to raise children, except the people who have them.
— P.J. O'Rourke

He looked me straight in the eyes, seemingly dumbfounded, as if he were unable to even comprehend what he'd just heard.

He then spent the next fifteen minutes not just telling me I was wrong, but berating me ruthlessly—red-faced, with veins popping out of his neck in anger. What happened that sent my friend Jack into such rage? Well, he had just learned of my decision to move my family to the Middle East to pursue a path of ministry. And he proceeded to give me a piece of his mind.

"How could you do this to your children?" Jack demanded. He waved his hand, gesturing to our surroundings. In his mind, this was an idyllic setting: a historic house in a National Park, an apple orchard, a grape arbor, deer as constant companions in our backyard, and a large, picturesque silver oak tree in the middle of it all. "How dare you force your kids to leave all this for some strange country?"

I stood there silently while Jack proceeded to tell me what a horrible parent I was. Then came the kicker. I remember his exact words.

"When your children end up on drugs, it will *all be your fault.*"

How do you respond to that?

Well, I didn't respond. Instead, I thanked him for his opinion and told him that I'd consider what he had said, which I think actually made him even more upset. Jack stomped off, still fuming, and I never saw him again. Unfortunately, he passed away while my family and I were overseas.

I'll admit that Jack did have a point. Our children, who were sixteen, fourteen, twelve, and ten at the time, did live in a pretty nice environment. And, as you will soon discover, creating a good environment is an important aspect of parenting. So, was I being a foolish parent, setting my children up for a bleak future strung out on drugs? The answer to this—and other questions—lies inside this book.

I share my encounter with Jack to help demonstrate that this book was not written from an ivory tower, nor is it a treatise on untested parenting theories. **The principles I'm about to share with you come from direct experience—for better *and* for worse.**

I sometimes joke that, by the world's standards, I've done just about everything wrong in parenting. Not only did my wife and I take our children overseas as planned, but they also lived in multiple countries and multiple states growing up. Two of our children finished high school while living apart from the family. Our kids have been home-schooled, public-schooled, and elite-private-schooled. Over the years, they've had lots of labels: "military brats," "pastor's kids," and "home-schoolers," just to name a few.

Our children still can't decide if they grew up rich or poor. At times, we had enough money to stay at resorts on the Red Sea. Other times, we were so poor that the stories from those days border on comical. Once, a deer ran in front of my car, and I had to lock the brakes to avoid hitting and killing the poor thing. Instead, it was my car who died; the old junker was so rusted that the force of the hard stop twisted and cracked the frame, and part of the engine tore loose. While sweet Bambi scampered away, the car went straight to the graveyard and was sold for scrap. (Can you imagine how my teenage children felt, being driven around in a car that could be killed by a deer?) Maybe Jack had more than one reason to berate me!

So how did *I* end up writing a book on parenting? And how did my kids *really* turn out?

One of the unique features of this book is that I will be sharing stories at the end of each chapter from the perspective of my children. They will tell you the same thing that is repeated throughout this book: that **my wife and I are not the perfect parents.** But we learned from the One who is. And it changed everything for us. Now, we have been blessed with the opportunity to watch it unfold as our children and their spouses apply these same principles as they raise our grandchildren.

I wasn't the perfect parent to my kids. I'm still not. But if you've read this far, then you might as well dive right in and learn from the One who *is* perfect—the One who can change your family in ways you never thought possible.

Chapter One:
There Is Hope

And hope does not disappoint.
Romans 5:5

For the hand that rocks the cradle is the hand that rules the world.
—William Ross Wallace

What am I supposed to do with this thing?

I'll never forget those words. They were the words running through my head as my wife Paula and I stared down at our newborn child on the day we brought him home from the hospital. Standing there, looking down at this amazing little creation in his crib, it suddenly hit us: After nine months of planning and preparation, we were parents.

What on Earth were we supposed to do now?

In case you're unaware, a newborn does not come with a handy instruction manual attached. A mother's journey through pregnancy is always the subject of a great deal of attention and excitement, and when that baby finally comes out and you're holding this naked little thing for the first time, it feels like the culmination of a lot of preparation and planning. In reality, it's only the beginning. And **most of us don't have a clue what to do next.**

I was no exception. When I first became a parent, it felt like I was flying blind.

I had little to no idea what it meant to be a good father. Many years prior, my dad had walked out on our family. As a result, I didn't have a solid example to follow. And so, looking down at my newborn child that day, I wondered, *How am I supposed to be a parent?*

Over the years, I've learned that many other parents ask themselves that same question, and there's no shortage of resources claiming to hold the answer. **Ask ten different people how to raise a child, and you'll get eleven different answers.** Go to the bookstore, and you'll find the Parenting section packed with titles promising to help you raise your child more effectively. Start browsing through them, however, and you'll quickly realize that they not only differ wildly in their advice but often *completely contradict* each other on many of the most basic fundamentals. So who really has the answer? What's a parent to do?

Naturally, many of us look for real-world, firsthand examples of how to raise children. When you see a well-rounded young adult with a good head on her shoulders, you start to wonder what her parents did right.

Maybe you were fortunate enough to have been blessed with parents who did it right. Perhaps they provided a wonderful example of what good parenting looks like. If so, congratulations! But don't celebrate just yet. **You were raised in a different time—** before cell phones, Netflix, social media, etc. The world is a very different place today than it was when you were a child. Your parents didn't face the kind of issues that *you* will face. They didn't need to worry about what age it was appropriate for you to have your first smartphone or to sign up for a Facebook account. What examples are out there for *you* to follow as a modern parent?

Spend a bit of time looking around, and you'll surely notice some patterns and recurring themes when it comes to parenting.

Three of the most popular methods, in particular, may catch your attention.

Parenting Method 1: The Yes Parent

Picture yourself in a restaurant, seated next to a family of three: a mother, a father, and a little girl.

The little girl looks like an angel. Yet she is rude to the waitress, talks back to her father, and has a meltdown when she's not allowed to order the biggest dessert on the menu. But it *works*. Despite all her bad behavior, Dad says, "Of course, honey," and before all is said and done, she's got that whopping dessert sitting in front of her.

The Yes Parent, also known as the *Permissive Parent*, says "yes" to almost anything their children ask of them. In their minds, always saying yes is what love looks like. They also tend to do a great job of justifying their yes answers to themselves and to those around them.

That little girl may hardly even touch her big expensive dessert. She may not have even been all that hungry! But she leaves the restaurant satisfied because she won the battle with her parents. From your table, you look on, determined not to allow *your* child to follow in those footsteps.

Parenting Method 2: The No Parent

On a sunny summer afternoon, you take your kids to the playground to work off a little energy. You're watching your children having fun when you spot a little boy sitting on a bench, seemingly afraid to move. You wonder to yourself, *Doesn't that boy want to go play with the other kids?*

After a moment, the little boy hesitantly moves toward the merry-go-round to join some of the other children, only for a stern-looking father to suddenly look up and bark a command like a drill sergeant: "Stay away from that thing! It's too dangerous for you." As you continue to watch, you notice that every move this little boy makes is met with disapproval. He might get hurt. He's not big enough. He's not old enough. The underlying message: He's *not good enough*.

The No Parent often self-identifies as a *Stern Parent*, and some of them actually take an awful lot of pride in this title. They may operate under the impression that they're acting in the best interests of their child, but the result of this *no*-first approach is a little boy who is scared to do anything but hover around the park bench with a sad look in his eye, constantly reminded of what he can't do, and thwarted at every step by his own father.

Those eyes haunt you. You shake your head at the drill sergeant father and vow to do anything in your power to prevent seeing that same look in *your* child's eyes.

Parenting Method 3: The What-Did-You-Say Parent

This parent is easy to spot. Let's say you take your daughter to her favorite fast-food restaurant. You know the one—it has a playground the size of a small amusement park attached to it. Your daughter loves climbing and sliding while you enjoy being able to take a moment to catch your breath from the busyness of parenting. But your daydreaming is interrupted by the sight of a little boy tugging on the shirt of the woman seated next to you. "Watch me, Mommy, watch me!" the little boy cries out. But the woman's eyes are locked on the screen of the phone in her hand. "Sure, honey," she replies half-heartedly. "Go ahead. I'm watching."

As you watch, the little boy runs off and goes inside the play area, turning to see if Mommy is, indeed, watching. But she's not. Her full attention is elsewhere. Her head is bowed as if in prayer to her almighty phone. The cycle begins: The boy runs back out and again asks Mommy to watch. Mommy mumbles, "Sure." The boy goes back in, and, sure enough, Mommy is still not paying attention. After a few rounds of this, the boy gives up and starts looking for friends who *will* pay attention to him.

The What-Did-You-Say Parent is, let's face it, the *Neglectful Parent*. These mothers and fathers often don't even realize what they're doing, let alone understand the effects of their behaviors, which can have devastating consequences.

You notice that the little boy is trying to latch on to the other kids, or maybe even other adults, in an effort to fulfill his need for attention—attention that is apparently lacking at home. You shudder as you put *your* phone away and lock your eyes on your daughter, vowing not to become a neglectful parent.

Do any of those three scenarios look familiar? Perhaps you've witnessed similar examples, or perhaps—ouch—you see a little of yourself in one of them.

Being a parent takes courage, and in this rapidly changing world, it's only getting harder. We all want to be the perfect parent to our children, but is such a thing even possible?

Fortunately, there's no need to despair. There is a perfect example worth following, and it's one you may have never considered before.

The Principles of the Perfect Parent

I think it's time I share a little about myself.

My name is Doug Ley. I have been a pastor for over fifteen years, and I was a professor in the Middle East for twelve years. I'm currently the President of Serving Beyond Borders, an Evangelical Spirit-filled ministry that seeks to equip and empower cross-cultural workers to advance the Gospel to the entire world. When not traveling, I also serve at a thriving church, training young men and women for ministry. But for the purposes of this book, it is most important to note that I am a husband, father, and grandfather, and I'm still madly in love with my wife Paula after thirty-seven years of marriage. We both love how the LORD has called and blessed our four children, and we watch with anticipation the blessings being poured out on our fifteen grandchildren (with the possibility of more to come!).

Part of my journey has been learning **the principles of Biblical parenting, as handed down by God through his Word.** In this book, I share God's parenting principles with you. And not just His principles, but better still, His *example* as the Perfect Parent.

Is God Good?

In his book *The Knowledge of the Holy,* A.W. Tozer wrote, "What comes to our minds when we think about God is the most important thing about us."

I'd like you to really think about this for a moment. What comes to *your* mind when you think about God?

Now, I know what you might be thinking. This is supposed to be a *parenting* book, not a book on theology! I get it. But in order to understand anything else I have to say, it's important that you first understand who God is. If you don't have a strong grasp on a bit of basic theology, you'll get lost.

So, who is God? Jesus taught us that if we've experienced salvation through Him, God is no longer just the God of Heaven, but He's our Heavenly Father. It's right there in the LORD's prayer—the second word of it, in fact. "Our **Father** who is in heaven." But do we think correctly about our Heavenly Father in this regard? I think that for many of us, the answer would, unfortunately, be *no*.

Is God good? Your willingness to accept the content I share with you in this book will depend on how you answer that question. Not just theoretically good; has He been good—even to you?

My doctorate is in apologetics. That means I seek to defend the Christian Faith against those who raise objections against it.[1] And there are *many* objections put forth against this Faith. But from my experience, the number one reason why people reject becoming a Christian is that they do not believe that there is a *good* God. They say things like, "How do you look at mass shootings and hurricanes and diseases and cancer, and believe that God is good?" In a world full of such evils, how *can* there be a good God?

When I first became a Christian, one of my high school friends had a sister who died of cancer. One day, I was witnessing to him,

---

[1] *Christian apologetics* may be simply defined as "the defense of the Christian Faith." See 1 Peter 3:15.

sharing Jesus with him, and he looked at me and said, "There is no God. If there is, why did He let my sister die?"

I can't deny that it's a valid question. How can there be a good God when there is so much messed up stuff in the world?

Back then, I didn't have an answer for my friend, but today, I know that the Bible is very clear on this. The Church needs to be very clear about it, too. **God is good.** In fact, Scripture supports this claim over and over again.

> *Oh give thanks to the LORD, for He is good, for*
> *His lovingkindness is everlasting.*
> **1 Chronicles 16:34**

Some define the word "lovingkindness" in the verse above as "mercy." It comes from the word *hesed* in Hebrew, which means "loyal love" or "covenant love." By the very definition of the word, **God is going to always love you,** and He's not going to break that love.

What Does "Heavenly Father" Mean?

Many people, when they hear that God is our "Father" or "the Heavenly Father," wonder what on Earth that means. Unfortunately, many of our misunderstandings stem from bad parenting here on Earth.

For many of us, negative images start to form. God's my Father, huh? Does that mean He's an angry, short-tempered bully? Does that mean He's going to beat me up and abuse me like my father did? Why doesn't God answer my prayers? It must be because He's like my earthly dad. Not around when I need Him. I guess I'll just have to figure it out on my own.

As I mentioned in the Introduction, I had a father who abandoned me. Some of you reading this may have had a similar experience. I know how easy it is to compare your Heavenly Father to your earthly one. I did it all the time!

But here's the thing: God is *never* going to abandon you.

God is never going to walk out of your life. His lovingkindness is everlasting. **He is good, but do you really believe that He is?**

Maybe you want to believe it. Maybe you even *say* that He is. But in your heart, do you really believe it?

If I had the chance to go back with the knowledge I have today and answer my high school friend's question, I would say, "Yes. Because of the Historic Fall and sin entering the world, cancer and death are real. But do you know anyone who is good enough to want to destroy cancer and powerful enough to do it? Just because the Creator God has not destroyed cancer and death **yet** does not mean He won't. In fact, from His revelation through His Son Jesus, He proved He is good through the healings and resurrections that Jesus performed. And He proved He is powerful enough by raising Jesus from the dead and giving Him power over death and sin. So, God is Good and will one day resurrect your sister, and through faith in Christ, you have hope of seeing her again."

Wow—that was a slight digression, but I feel it was necessary because God is always getting a bad rap for all the evil in the world. Pay attention, and you'll notice that the same people complaining about Him never seem to have an answer to the problems we're in. But that's a topic for another day. . . .

"If God is so good," you may be saying to yourself, "then why am I in the circumstances that currently plague my life?"

Let's follow Scripture and test this to figure it out.

O taste and see that the LORD is good; how
blessed is the one who takes refuge in Him!

Psalm 34:8

Have you tasted and seen how good the LORD is? I want you to think about that question as you proceed through this book.

The goodness of our Heavenly Father is just an introduction to who He is, and your answer to this key question is indicative of whether or not you have experienced His true nature.

A simple mistake in your thinking may be hindering you from being the parent you want to be.

What is Your Goal?

A dream is just a dream. A goal is a dream
with a plan and a deadline.

—Harvey Mackay

Parenting isn't all sunshine and rainbows. Sometimes, it can feel more like traversing a minefield; one false move, and things blow up in your face. In the middle of such a seemingly treacherous journey, it's natural to seek advice, but **you must be discerning about the source**.

Many parents, in their quest for help, will at some point seek advice from licensed counselors or professional therapists. My response to this approach is, "Okay, but have you ever seen *their* children?"

Why would you seek counsel from someone just because they have an advanced degree? There are psychiatrists and psychologists who have completely dysfunctional families, yet people pay them $200 an hour to get their opinion!

I'm all for seeking advice from someone—*if* they have the type of family worth emulating. But even then, can they guarantee that the goals you have for your child will be met by following their philosophy?

Before we look at the example set by our Heavenly Father, we need to understand a key principle in life: **Without a goal, you cannot score.**

What's your goal as a parent? This may strike you as a strange question, and if you've never really thought about it before, you're not alone. The majority of parents raise their children without any clear goals, blindly hoping their children turn out right. Others have goals, but their goals are so narrow and unrealistic that no child, no matter how good, could ever reach them. Finally, there are the parents who have clear goals that are achievable, but the focus is on the incorrect aspect of the desired outcome. Thus, the child might attain their educational goal but fail the character test miserably, becoming an ethical disaster even though their place in their career field is to be envied.

So, what is the goal of parenting? Again, this question, like the overall question of this book, "how do I raise my child correctly?" is subjective from a human perspective. It is based on one's personal opinion, and the answer may vary wildly depending on the individual. However, if we turn our gaze to a transcendental perspective—one that goes beyond human opinion and arguments—then there is hope. Hope that the effort we place in raising our children will be worth it, not only in this world but also in the one to come.

In his book *Parenting by The Book*, John Rosemond provides an illustration of a woman who chose a parenting method that suited *her* best, rather than choosing what would have been best for her child. As Rosemond pointed out to this mother, "The matter of how a child should be raised is not about the parent; it's about the child."[2]

Too many parents make the goal of parenting about them. And if that's the case, they will want the easiest, least time-consuming, most convenient way of parenting, even though it might not be what's best for the child. This is a critical error.

The goal of parenting must start with what's best for the child. And if that's the goal, we then have to ask, who has the authority to tell us what's best? This is another key question that every parent must ask.

Finding Direction

> *O LORD. . . . Build me a son whose heart will be clear, whose goal will be high, a son who will master himself before he seeks to master other men, one who will reach into the future, yet never forget the past.*
> **—General Douglas MacArthur**

One night, Paula and I were invited to Rob and Donna's house for dinner. It was thirty-three years ago, yet I remember like it was yesterday.

Rob and Donna were friends of ours who had three boys ranging from thirteen to eight years old. Naturally, we walked in

---

[2] John K. Rosemond, *Parenting by The Book*, NY: Howard Books, 2007, 1

expecting a circus. Instead, we were shocked when these boys walked up to us, introduced themselves, looked us in the eyes, and gave us firm handshakes.

Rob and Donna's boys were polite and gladly took our children into the next room and played kindly with them. They even helped serve dinner and clean the table. Frankly, Paula and I were amazed. We had never seen such well-behaved children. As we drove home that night, we reminisced over everything that had amazed us about their children. Clearly, Rob and Donna had some parenting secret. We knew instantly that we needed to learn it and apply it in our family.

Within a few weeks, we had Rob and Donna over to our home. There, we fired the question at them, point-blank, before they even had a chance to get settled in: "What's the key to raising children like yours?" We were hungry to learn, and fortunately for us, they were eager to teach.

Rob didn't beat about the bush. He got right to the point. "We simply follow the Bible."

That's it? I wondered. *That's the secret sauce? No way. He's not telling me the full story! There must be more to it than that.*

But yes, that was the whole story.

Rob and Donna explained that all their parenting decisions were based on the Bible. They spoke to their children the way the Bible said to speak. They disciplined their children according to the Biblical description of discipline. They instilled a work ethic in them as described in the Bible. The answers were all right there, waiting for us to act on them.

It was as if a lightbulb came on in our minds. If the Bible is the Word of God, then why not seek out what It says about raising children? And so began our adventure of searching the Bible to see what it said about parenting. Before long, we discovered that there was more to learn than we ever would have guessed.

Didactic teaching is great, and we soon realized that the Bible was full of clear instructions on parenting. We looked up verses, wrote them down, studied them, and sought to apply them (for your benefit, I've included a list of Bible verses on aspects of parenting in the appendix of this book). It helped, but while commands, proverbs, and parables are great, something was still missing—a final piece of the puzzle from the Bible to help us in our quest to become good parents.

Finding the Answer

I don't know who my grandfather was; I am more concerned to know what his grandson will be.

—Abraham Lincoln

Have you ever had one of those moments when you're desperately searching for something, only to find that it was right there in front of your face the whole time? Ask and you shall receive.

At the beginning of this chapter, I mentioned that God, as defined by Jesus, is our Heavenly Father. Well, for years, I have lived by the motto, "No Bible, no breakfast." I start the day seeking the LORD through study and prayer. And when I pray, I begin by reciting the LORD's Prayer. If you're a Christian or you grew up in the Church, you probably know the LORD's Prayer by heart, but let's take a look at the words:

Our Father in Heaven, hallowed be Your Name, Your Kingdom come, Your will be done, on earth as it is in Heaven. Give us today our daily bread. And forgive us our debts, as we have forgiven our debtors. And lead us not into temptation, but deliver us from the evil one.

For many Christians, the LORD's Prayer has become a routine set of words, often recited with little reflection of what's actually being said. But the LORD's Prayer is incredibly powerful. Lest we forget, this is the model of prayer that Jesus personally gave to His followers.

One day, I woke up and—no Bible, no breakfast—sat down to seek the LORD. As usual, I began with the LORD's Prayer. But this time, I didn't get past the second word.

"Our Father. . . ."

Our Father.

Father. . . . Of course! That was it!

All at once, I had my answer. Not only did God's Word contain instructions on how to be a parent, but it provided a living, all-powerful example of what the one and only *perfect* parent looks like. The example of how to be a good father had been right in front of me the entire time. God isn't just the Creator of the Universe, the All-Knowing, All-Powerful One. He's also our Heavenly Father.

God is a parent—the Perfect Parent.

So began a study that became the foundation for how Paula and I raised our children. We simply looked at how our Heavenly Father raised His first created children, Adam and Eve. We compared His example with the teachings throughout Scripture to see how they lined up. The book in your hands is the result of that study.

In that moment, I had clarity. God told me, "I'm your Heavenly Father. Look to Me on how to be a parent." This insight was the starting point.

Over time, God led me to five key principles on Biblical parenting, right out of the book of Genesis—principles flowing from God that He used to parent His first child, Adam. And, after a lot of study and a lot of prayer, my wife and I made the decision to live by these principles **to pastor, minister, and love our children the same way that God pastors, ministers, and loves us as His children.**

God isn't just a good parent. He's *the* one and only *Perfect Parent.*

The Five Principles

Obey the principles without being bound by them.

—Bruce Lee

Before we proceed any further, there's something I must say, and I can't stress this enough:

I am *not* the perfect parent. Only He is.

It's easy to write a book and make it all sound so simple and easy. But that's not reality. Parenting is messy, and I intend to be transparent with you in the coming pages regarding our shortcomings in raising our children. Our kids had tantrums, disobeyed, broke things, hid things, fought with each other. In fact, they were kids! And as parents, we also had our fair share of tantrums. We disobeyed our own rules, broke things (not the kids!), hid things, and fought. In fact, we were human!

At times, all of us have made mistakes in our parenting. Nobody is perfect except for the LORD. Even the best are bound to fall.

My kids have seen behind the curtain; they've seen me at my best as a parent and at my worst. Today, they all live radical, fulfilling lives, for which I am eternally grateful, and Paula and I, to our delight, are seeing the fruits of the principles outlined in this book being passed on to the next generation. We take no credit for this. We take credit only in God's Word because God is faithful to His promises.

In this book, I will share **the Five Principles of how to be a good parent, learned through my studies of *the* Perfect Parent.** This book is primarily about Godly parenting, but it's also about principles that can be applied across a broad spectrum. If you're the owner of a company, a supervisor, a coach, or a person in any other position of influence, implement these five principles and watch a positive shift take place.

While reading, you may at times feel uncomfortable. But embrace the learning process. I promise you, like a surgeon skillfully yielding a scalpel to bring about healing, so the instruction of the LORD will bring healing to the confusion and conflicts that arise from the dilemma of raising children in this rapidly changing society.

My goal is for you to see these five principles *in the context of relationship*. I could have just written the principles as "Five Keys to Raising Perfect Kids" or "Five Steps to Raising Successful Kids." And while this is what a marketing guru would advocate, it is not what Scripture does. Instead, we find in God's Word an example through which to see the principles fleshed out.

In short, these are *principles*, not laws or formulas. By seeing the principles and the perfect example, you will be equipped to apply them in the context of your own relationship with your children. That's the beauty of seeing the Perfect Parent.

Once you've determined in your mind that God is good, that He loves you, and that He wants the best for you, then you can learn from Him how to be a good parent.

And so, without any further introduction, let's get into it and learn the Five Principles of the Perfect Parent.

The Five Principles of the Perfect Parent

The Perfect Parent:
1. Creates a Good Environment for His Children
2. Gives Responsibility to His Children
3. Sets Boundaries for His Children
4. Keeps His Word and Disciplines His Children
5. Does Everything in Love and Always Shows His Love

In the following chapters, we'll examine each of these principles in detail.

The Five Principles in Action

The problem with a lot of books on parenting is that you don't get the full story. After all, if you're going to accept anything that I have to say on the subject of parenting, wouldn't it be good to hear things from *my* kids' point of view?

To help bring to light the true impact of the Five Principles, I asked my editor to interview my adult children so we could share their perspectives at the end of each chapter in this book. This serves the dual purpose of providing real-life examples of how the Five Principles affected their lives and showing that my wife and I really did practice what I'm preaching in these pages.

In the following chapters, you'll hear from my four kids: Jacob, Joshua, Bethany, and Josiah. I've asked them to be honest and candid in sharing their thoughts because I think it's important that you, as the reader, have an opportunity to realize that these principles were learned through the grace of the LORD.

Jacob

Jacob is the oldest and has been married to his wife Alicia for over thirteen years. They have two biological sons (eleven and nine years old at the time of this writing) and an older adopted daughter. He actually has two grandchildren, too (which technically makes me a great-grandfather!). Jacob is a pastor in Farmington Hills, Michigan.

"My parents had me in their early twenties," says Jacob, "and I grew up, in a lot of ways, as my parents were still maturing into adulthood themselves. One of the things I've taken from my parents is to not be passive as a parent but to lean toward intentionality. They were truly intentional in teaching us Biblical principles growing up. I've also come to realize over the years that part of parenting comes out of individual personality—your own personality as well as the personalities of your children."

Joshua

Joshua has been married to his wife Ali for over thirteen years. They have six children, ages ten, eight, five, three, and one. Joshua is an officer in the United States Marine Corps. At the time of this writing, he is stationed in Japan.

"Our parents put a huge investment into us as children in terms of quality time, which I think has made all the difference," says Joshua. "The only way to grow relationships and establish trust is with time. I'll be honest, things weren't always perfect. My parents were busy people, and there was sometimes tension, especially during the ministry years in Egypt (more on that later), but the principles they instilled in us have stood the test of time."

Bethany

Bethany and her husband Johan have been married for over twelve years. She is a consummate homemaker and is currently living in the Netherlands. She and Johan have five children, ages ten, eight, seven, five, and one.

"I learned from my parents that a relationship with Jesus must be at the center of everything," says Bethany. "I also learned that parenting is a relationship-based process. It's not surprising to me that the first chapter of this book is about the fundamentals of sound theology. In my own journey as a parent, I have come to realize that if I'm not in the Word and in an active relationship with the LORD, my parenting suffers. Like my dad (whom I've always called 'Took'), I try to be intentional with my children."

Josiah

Josiah has been married to his wife Larissa for over seven years. They have two kids: a three-year-old and a one-year-old. He works in the non-profit sector and lives in Houston, Texas.

"My parents modeled humility in that they wanted us, their children, to do better than them in every single aspect of their lives," says Josiah. "There was always a high degree of accountability. We've had some brokenness, but thanks to the principles my parents taught us, we can always come back to Jesus as a unifying place where we rally."

Self-Assessment Questions

Each chapter of this book will conclude with a series of self-assessment questions that are designed to get you thinking and primed for Godly change. I encourage you to write down your answers. No cheating—be brutally honest with yourself.

1. Have you personally seen examples of the "Yes Parent," the "No Parent," or the "What-did-you-say Parent"? How do you feel about the examples that come to mind?

2. How have the examples in Question 1 influenced your views on parenting (positively and/or negatively)?

3. Do you truly believe that God is Good? Why or why not?

4. What are your goals in parenting? Spend some time reflecting, then write down four to six specific goals you have for your children.

Chapter Two:
Principle One: Create a Good Environment

God saw all that He had made, and behold, it was very good.

Genesis 1:31

There is no place like home.
—**L. Frank Baum**

If you spend some time in the first few chapters of the Book of Genesis, you'll quickly notice the same phrase being repeated: "It was good."

Day One, and it was good. Day Three[3], and it was good. And so on and so forth. And at the end of that first week:

> *God saw all that He had made, and behold, it was very good. And there was evening and there was morning, the sixth day.*

---

[3] There is much discussion as to why Day Two does not use this phrase, while Day Three uses it two times. I am convinced, since all Scripture points to Jesus (John 5:46; Luke 24:27, 44), that this is a picture of the Gospel (1 Cor. 15:1-6), that Jesus is the Christ, who died for our sins and was buried and in the ground on the Second Day, meaning it is not a blessed day. But He rose from death to life on the Third Day, which gives it a double blessing as typology in Creation. But let's save that discussion for another book!

In Hebrew, the phrase "very good" is emphatic here. This was something special that God had created.

Do we still believe that today? In spite of all the messed-up stuff in this world, **do you believe that God created it good?**

The world has twisted this around through the widespread acceptance of the theory of atheistic evolution. We are told that the world was *never* perfect, especially not at the beginning—that death and killing have always existed, and that we are just random-chance creatures who evolved by exploiting certain elements of this imperfect environment. The underlying message of this worldview is that life is pointless.

Western society is living beneath the legacy of this deadly philosophy, and the effects are beginning to show. And then we wonder why so many people are falling deeper and deeper into depression. If there's no meaning in life, why continue on living? Depression is up, suicide rates are up, all forms of abuse are up, and few people are willing to look at the cause and face the reality of what has shifted in society in the last one hundred years.

If we're not created in God's image—*if we're just animals*—then who cares? What's the point? In the end, it's all meaningless anyway.

This is a lie.

The Bible paints a very different picture. God is good, and we see this at the very beginning because God created everything good. But the lie of imperfection has crept into the Church, and it's been alarming to me to see it sweeping through the collective mentality of believers.

The Church needs to stop this lie.

Yes, this is a fallen world. Yes, there is evil in it. But God is good, and He created it good! And because of that fact, **I can have true hope that it's going to be good in the end.**

We *know* that it's going to be better in the end. We have hope. The Church needs to tell the world that we have the answer. If God created it good in the beginning, He can recreate it good in the end.

God Created It Good—and So Should We!

No work is insignificant. All labor that uplifts humanity has dignity and importance and should be undertaken with painstaking excellence.

—Martin Luther King Jr.

In 1950, sociologists Sheldon and Eleanor Glueck of Harvard University published a controversial landmark study proposing that a set of four basic factors could predict, with no less than 90 percent accuracy, whether children as young as six years old would become delinquent.[4] Those four factors were:

1. The father's discipline (it must be firm and consistent)
2. The mother's supervision
3. The father and mother's affection for each other
4. The family's cohesiveness (spending time together)

---

[4] Glueck, S., & Glueck, E. (1950). Unraveling Juvenile delinquency. Commonwealth Fund.

Interestingly, these findings align with Biblical Parenting Principle #1: **Create a good environment for your children**.

From the beginning, God created a good environment. This is the clear teaching of Genesis 1. If we are to follow His example, we must also create a good environment for our children. But what exactly do I mean by creating a "good" environment?

I once heard a pastor say that he always judged sermons by three little letters: *YBH*. YBH stands for "yes, but how?" I soon grasped the importance of these letters, not just in sermons but in life.

So, should we create a good environment for our children? Yes. But... *how*?

What Does a Good Environment Look Like?

> *There is something quite beautiful about the Grand Canyon at night. There is something beautiful about a billion stars held steady by a God who knows what He is doing.*
> **—Donald Miller**

I don't know about you, but all my life, it felt like society was telling me to go to school, get a job, and make money.

With that money, we are supposed to get a big house, drive a nice car, send our kids to the best schools, and give them all the best stuff. That is the American Dream, and many have bought into it. And with that, many believe that *this* is how you create a good environment for your children. Unfortunately, it's yet another materialistic, worldly lie that has hurt many a family.

Men and women spend their entire lives operating under an incorrect assumption that if they give their children the environment described above, everything will be great! And then they wonder why their kids rebel and reject their teaching and upbringing.

Parents work all their lives to send their son to the best college, and then they are bewildered when he flunks out because all he does is get high every day. He had everything going for him—every advantage. This sort of scenario happens all the time. Why does this happen?

Well, it might be because this wayward son was raised in a not-so-good environment.

A plant raised in a poor environment, with bad soil, little sunlight, and no water, will eventually wither away. So, too, will a son or daughter wither due to the soil in which they are planted. I'm not saying there's anything right or wrong about going to the best school, having the best clothes, or living in a nice house. But that's not the kind of "good environment" we're talking about.

There is a way to create a good environment for your children, and the steps come straight from Scripture.

Speak Words of Life in Your Home

If I hadn't opened my big mouth, I wouldn't be here.

**—Sign under a fish
mounted on a wall**

Evangelist Bill Glass, who did prison ministry for many years, is reported to have once asked a group of 1,000 prison inmates the following question: "How many of you had parents who told you that you would end up in prison one day?" Almost every one of the inmates raised his hand. This alone should illustrate the power of the words we choose to speak to (and over) our children.

Now, let me ask, what kind of words are spoken in your house? The Bible tells us there are only two types of words we can speak: Words of Life or Words of Death.

Proverbs 18:21 reads, "Death and life are in the power of the tongue. . . ." That's it. So, do you speak words that bring life to others? Do you encourage, lift up, promote, or build up others? The parents of the aforementioned prisoners appear to have chosen to speak Words of Death[5] over their sons. Clearly, we need to be very careful here. **What you say in your family can affect your children negatively or positively for their entire lives.**

---

[5] We call these WODs (pronounced *wads*) in our family. To break our habit of saying these, we trained ourselves to just say "WOD" when someone slipped and said a Word of Death. We received quite a few odd stares in public, but it worked!

Sticks and Stones

Many years ago, my wife and I were having dinner with some of our extended family members. I was talking with the patriarch of the family, a man well into his seventies. I asked the man how he'd met his wife, a lovely lady who was serving him and the family while still working a full-time job as a teacher. He laughed and said, "It was the darkest day of my life."

How sad.

Was he just making a joke? Maybe. But think about what that comment communicated—not only to this man's wife, but to their children about their mother. And about marriage in general.

Perhaps it should come as no surprise that I ended up conducting marriage counseling with this man's son and his wife. This man's son was a product of Words of Death in the home that had been passed down to him.

That wasn't the only story told that night. Another man at the table felt compelled to tell me about how his daughter had been overweight as a little girl. He related how one day, while playing at a park, she had gotten stuck in a climbing tube, and all the kids had made fun of her. Her father told me this story over dinner, in front of the entire family. Here was this lovely thirty-something-year-old lady, listening to her father tell this story. The look in her eyes said it all. Again, it shouldn't surprise you to learn that this woman still struggled with an eating disorder and problems with her body image.

In many houses, nothing is ever good enough. The grades are never good enough. The kids are never smart enough. They're not practicing enough. And, perhaps most caustic of all, children are told they're not as good as their brothers or sisters. In this embattled, embittered, dog-eat-dog environment, kids can't wait to get away!

An extreme example of this came up fairly recently. I was speaking at a church, and I started talking about the contrast between a family that speaks Words of Life versus one that speaks Words of Death. When I mentioned how Words of Death commonly take the form of comparing one sibling to another, I noticed a woman out of the corner of my eye who had become visibly shaken. She put her head down and started muttering something under her breath.

As I continued, I said, "And one of the worst things you can do is to say Words of Death over someone's physical appearance or compare their looks to someone else's." At that moment, I thought this woman was going to come unglued. She waited anxiously for the sermon to end and then practically ran up to me as soon as I stepped away from the stage.

"That's right, you're exactly right," she blurted out. "My mother was always telling me I was the ugly one and that I'd never be as pretty as my sister. I lived with that my whole life. Is it any wonder I ended up a drug addict and a prostitute?"

At this point, she grew quite agitated and began muttering to herself again, so I looked at her and started speaking Words of Life into her. She was sobbing at this point. She knew God loved her, and she told me she had committed her life to Jesus Christ, accepting His forgiveness for all the wrong she had done. But forgiving her mother? Well, now we were pushing her beyond her comfort zone.

I would love to say that we had an incredible time of healing and freedom right there. But that's not what happened. She left with a state of war in her mind. She knew she needed not only to accept that God loved her just as she was at that moment, but also to forgive her mother. But **Words of Death are like splinters in the mind and require a powerful encounter with God to remove them.**

Although this is a book on parenting, perhaps there's someone you need to forgive right now. It may be the very thing preventing you from experiencing a breakthrough in your parenting. As Nelson Mandela said, "Not forgiving others is like drinking poison and expecting the other person to die." Don't let bitterness be passed on to your children just because you are unwilling to forgive someone who hurt you or spoke a Word of Death to you. Unfortunately for the woman in the story, she just couldn't let go yet.

I can't help but think back to a highly publicized experiment conducted by an elementary school teacher who shared with her pupils that scientific reports had verified that children with blue eyes had greater natural learning abilities than children with brown eyes. She had them make up little signs designating themselves as blue eyes or brown eyes, which they then hung around their necks.

After a week or so, the achievement levels of the brown-eyed students fell measurably, while the performance of the blue-eyed students improved significantly. She then made a startling announcement to the class. She had made a mistake! It was the blue-eyed people who were the weaker students and the brown-eyed ones who were the stronger students. Surprise, surprise—up went the self-image and academic achievement of the brown-eyed group, and down came the performance of the blue-eyed children. The teacher then presented the results of this experiment to the kids' mothers and fathers as a lesson in parenting.

Never underestimate the power of a spoken word.

Cultivate Peace

Peace begins with a smile.

—Mother Teresa

In the Garden of Eden, there was no conflict or fighting. And as Paula and I further devoted ourselves to parenting God's way, we decided that, as parents, we were going to set the tone for the house.

No fighting, period.

That's right. None. If my wife and I had a disagreement, we didn't hash it out in front of the children. Likewise, we didn't let our kids talk back to us, throw tantrums, cause disruptions in the home, fight, or pick on their siblings.

Naturally, our kids tested us in this. It's part of their human nature. Yes, our two-year-olds would still throw themselves on the ground as if they'd been shot, screaming at the tops of their lungs. But they quickly learned that this was unacceptable in our house.

Is your house a house of peace? Or is it a warzone? Perhaps you've become so accustomed to Words of Death and fighting that you don't even sense the constant tension in the room. But I guarantee you, **your children sense it.**

Hit the Deck!

Have you ever been with a couple when the WODs started flying?

You know the sort of fight I'm talking about—while out to eat at a restaurant, the man will make a comment like, "Wow, this food is fantastic. I wish *you* could cook like this." His wife then rises to the negative challenge: "Well, if you brought home enough money to buy food like this, then perhaps my cooking would improve." And so the war begins.

I've been in those situations. Most of us want to put our heads down and hope the verbal bullets fly over us as we silently eat our meals. But at some point, I decided that I was no longer going to put my head down. Instead, I would confront the war head-on.

In these situations, my policy is to point out the Words of Death that are being spoken. I seek to help the couple see a blind spot in their relationship. But often, both parties will just stare at me, dumbfounded. They have been fighting so regularly for so long that they don't even hear what they sound like. And they certainly can't sense the tension they've created around them. To paraphrase Jeremiah 17:9, people have a great capacity to lie to themselves and think it's all right.

Has this silent killer invaded *your* home and ruined the good environment you desire for your children? Are your children living with tension that they were never meant to live with?

I would encourage you to have an honest conversation with yourself and, if possible, with your spouse. Ask another couple, someone whom you are friends with, if they think your house is peaceful or if there is tension in it. Your children's future is worth doing whatever it takes to raise them in a good environment.

A Message to Single Parents

Unfortunately, the unique issues facing single parents aren't often discussed in church; anytime there's a series on parenting, the single parents tend to get overlooked. This is extremely unfair.

Divorced parents, especially, walk a tough road. If this describes you, you may have found yourself reading the previous section and wondering, how are you supposed to follow the principles of love and respect for the father or mother of your children when they're not even around? How are you supposed to speak Words of Life to someone like that?

Single parents, you have it hard. Trying to raise a child on your own is an incredible challenge. But let me say this: I don't care if your ex-husband is the antichrist or your ex-wife is the Wicked Witch of the West incarnate: **Never speak a Word of Death about that ex in front of your children**. No matter who they are, that man or that woman is still the parent of that child, and you need to speak Words of Life into that.

Don't get me wrong—I know how hard it is. I know your child comes home from spending the weekend with your ex-spouse and tells you, "You know what dad says about you?" But no matter what the other parent might be saying, your response to your child needs to be, "We are going to pray that God grabs hold of your dad's heart and helps him."

Even if what you're really thinking in your head is, "God, I wish you would grab that man's *throat* and choke him," don't you say it! Because, listen to me, parent: **Truth and time go hand in hand**.

One day, your child is going to be old enough and wise enough to look back and know that *you* took the high road. That *you* spoke life. They'll know the truth. And that will give them a foundation on which they can stand.

How to Speak Words of Life

I immediately fell in love with the following story when I first heard it. I use it in almost every talk I give on the power of speaking Words of Life to children. It is called *The Whisper Test* by Mary Ann Bird.[6] She writes:

> *I grew up knowing I was different, and I hated it. I was born with a cleft palate, and when I started school, my classmates made it clear to me how I looked to others: a little girl with a misshapen lip, crooked nose, lopsided teeth and garbled speech.*
>
> *When schoolmates asked, "What happened to your lip?" I'd tell them I'd fallen and cut it on a piece of glass. Somehow it seemed more acceptable to have suffered an accident than to*

---

[6] This story is found in many books and countless sermon illustrations. Finding its original source has proven elusive. However, the following article does seem to support the authenticity of the story. See "On Compassion: The Whisper Test" in *Leaders Helps*, https://leaderhelps.com/2017/02/06/on-compassion-the-whisper-test/ (accessed on 3/28/2020).

*have been born different. I was convinced that
no one outside my family could love me.*

*There was, however, a teacher in the second
grade whom we all adored—Mrs. Leonard by
name. She was short, round, happy—a
sparkling lady.*

*Annually we had a hearing test. . . . Mrs.
Leonard gave the test to everyone in the class,
and finally it was my turn. I knew from past
years that as we stood against the door and
covered one ear, the teacher sitting at her desk
would whisper something, and we would have
to repeat it back—things like, "The sky is blue,"
or, "Do you have new shoes?" I waited there for
those words that God must have put into her
mouth, those seven words that changed my life.
Mrs. Leonard said, in her whisper, "I wish you
were my little girl."*

This is a great illustration of how one Word of Life can change
a person's heart. **Words of Life are powerful and need to be
spoken over our children continuously.**

God says to every person deformed by sin, "I wish you were my
son" or, "I wish you were my daughter." And He demonstrated
the truth of those Words of Life by sending Christ to do
something about our sin.

> *But God demonstrates His own love toward us,*
> *in that while we were yet sinners, Christ died*
> *for us.*
>
> **Romans 5:8**

We can imitate the Perfect Parent.

Fathers, take control of your house and speak life into it. Purge the bickering and the complaining from it. Work hard to provide a stable physical environment.

Mothers, take control of the situation and speak life into it. Correct negative talk and banish it from your home. Work hard to make sure that your children will not have to grow up too fast but can be children while you provide and care for them.

Our home was dedicated to being a place where calm reigned, not chaos. This takes work, but it's worth it.

Now is the time for you to turn your house into a home.

The Five Principles in Action

Jacob

"I remember growing up in an environment that felt very *intentional*. My parents always took the time to explain things to us in a loving and affirming way. With that came certain expectations, as well as some structure regarding what our home environment ought to be like.

"We were home-schooled until I was in eighth grade, but my parents taught us to be independent learners and to take responsibility in that. We were allowed and encouraged to learn things for ourselves, make mistakes, and figure things out as we went."

Joshua

"Words of Life were spoken in our home, and I never remember my parents fighting. I don't remember conflict in the home. The downside to this, I think, is that it didn't teach us conflict resolution, but you could always count on our home being a peaceful place.

"One thing that stands out is that there was a high priority placed on quality time just for Mom and Dad to be together. I think this is incredibly important. At our house in Ohio, we had a big tree that we called the 'Tree of Life,' where Mom and Dad would sit and have coffee together every day. I understood from a young age that while quality time with us was important, they also needed time when it was just the two of them. The message was, 'We are not Mommy and Daddy right now; we are Husband and Wife.' I saw that my parents loved one another even more than they loved us. Today, my kids know the same thing. They know that their mom is my top priority."

Bethany

"My memories are of a household where peace and quality time were considered very important. My parents kept the peace. They didn't argue in front of us. They hashed things out behind closed doors.

"I have memories of Mom cooking while I played games with Dad. He worked a lot, but he did a great job of being involved when he was home. I always felt like family was a huge priority to all of us, especially in the elementary-age years.

"I also *never* felt that we kids were a burden. We were an enjoyable part of our parents' lives, and they were creative about making family time for us to spend together. When we traveled, they always made sure we got a hotel with a pool so we could have fun. The time we spent together helped build strong, lasting relationships."

Josiah

"Safety, fun, and peace are what come to my mind when I think of our family's environment. While there was a lot of accountability in our house, we also had a lot of freedom. My parents trusted us with a lot and created a fun environment at home. Mom was creative and engaging, and Dad always made time, especially in those younger years, to engage with us, whether that meant playtime or wrestling.

"My parents created an environment where we *wanted* things to be peaceful. Just about every night, we spent quality time together. And there was a real feeling that our parents were investing in us, teaching us, and passing on talents."

Self-Assessment Questions

1. God created a good environment for His children. Besides those stated in this chapter, what other ways can parents help create a good environment for their children?

2. Did you grow up in a house where Words of Life or Words of Death were spoken? How has that shaped the environment you are now creating for your children?

3. Can you think of a time when a situation would have been different if you had chosen to speak Words of Life?

4. Would you describe your house as a house of peace? Why or why not?

Chapter Three:
Principle Two: Give Responsibility

*Then the LORD God took the man and put him
in the Garden of Eden to cultivate it and keep
it.*

Genesis 2:15

The price of greatness is responsibility.
—Winston Churchill

We've all heard the stories. Frustrated fathers and mothers who have their thirty-something-year-old son or daughter still living with them, not looking for a job, playing on their phones all day. Well, if this scenario is your goal, the following is a sure-fire recipe.[7]

Principle 1: Begin with infancy to give the child everything he wants.

Principle 2: When he picks up bad words, laugh at him.

Principle 3: Never give him any spiritual training. Wait until he's twenty-one years old, and then let him "decide for himself."

Principle 4: Avoid using the word "wrong." It may cause him to develop a guilt complex.

---

[7] The original source for this "recipe" is unknown, although years ago, it was distributed by the Houston Police Department under the title *Twelve Rules for Raising Delinquent Children.*

Principle 5: Pick up everything he leaves lying around, so he will be experienced in casting responsibility on everybody else.

If the adult child I just described is your idea of the product of successful parenting, then feel free to close this book now. You already have everything you need to know. If not, then I encourage you to keep reading. God has more to say on this matter.

Responsibility Defined

Too often our failure to commit our own young people to our own cause leads to their subsequent defection. We fear that we shall risk too much if we make demands upon them, and we lose all as a consequence.

—Douglas Hyde

A surprise awaits many parents who begin to study God's example of parenting. Many are taken aback to discover that God gave **work** to Adam *before* sin entered the world, not after it.

That's right. God put the humans in the Garden and told them to *work*. Adam and Eve were to cultivate the Garden and keep it.

People seem to think that work is part of the "curse" of this fallen world. This is yet another misguided philosophy that has crept into our Christian thinking.

In reality, the first thing God gave Adam was responsibility. Even before Eve came on the scene, God had already put Adam to work, and that's what we as Christians are supposed to do. **We are** *supposed* **to work.**

We are supposed to go out into the world and make it better. But have you listened recently to how people talk about work? Most people *hate* work. The false narrative from media and advertising promotes dreaming about the weekend or that fantasy vacation or that day when we can retire and work no more. In short, **modern society glorifies leisure**. And as a result, people become slaves to this false narrative and slog through life working at jobs they hate, their eyes fixed on what they perceive to be the ideal end result. Is it any wonder that many young people view work with disdain, or that they change jobs every couple of years? As a popular song of the '90s said, "My mother says to get a job, but she don't like the one she got." Hypocrisy always shows itself.

But God knows us better than we know ourselves. That's why we need to follow His example in parenting and not that of the world. He knows, and research confirms, that a child who is given responsibility is more likely to be a contributor versus a consumer. But a child left on his own tends to self-destruct and do harm instead of good in this world. As the Proverb says, a child left to himself brings shame to his parents (Proverbs 29:15).

Responsibility Equals Stewardship

"You cannot teach a child to take care of himself unless you will let him try. He will make mistakes; and out of these mistakes will come his wisdom."

—Henry Ward Beecher

Here was Adam in paradise. Beautiful landscape, the lushest plants to eat from, a pristine river to swim and refresh himself. All one could hope for. But God knew this wasn't enough. If Adam was going to flourish in this paradise, he needed to take responsibility for it. He was *to cultivate it and keep it*, the Bible says.

Do you know people who are part of a group that isolates from the world? The ones who huddle together and try to get away from the big bad world and hide in little sanctuaries of their own making? They judge the world but don't seem to be trying to improve it. That is *so opposite* of how it should be!

As obedient children of our Heavenly Father, **we must embrace work and heed the responsibility to get out there and make things better**. We are called to be the creative geniuses who help make this life a better place to live. We do that as children of God, and we teach that as parents to our children.

We have, of course, learned from this. We are not to make our children start working for a living as child laborers, but we have also learned the principle from God: *Give your children responsibilities.*

Do you give your child responsibility? Or do you do everything for them? Too many parents are under the impression that creating a good environment for a child means acting like their personal servants. They wash their clothes, cook their food, clean their room, etc. This is the opposite of the example set by our Father in Heaven.

Don't Lose Heart

If you want your children to keep their feet on the ground, put some responsibility on their shoulders.

—**Abigail Van Buren**

When my family and I lived in the Middle East, we moved into a house used by a former missionary. With it, we inherited Margret, a domestic worker who cleaned the house once a week. We never found out Margret's real age, but to say she was getting into the twilight years of her life would be a kind way of saying it. We really didn't want a domestic worker, but it was all the income Margret had, and she sent most of it back to her country to care for her extended family.

We grew to love Margret, and she us. But most of all, she loved our youngest son, Josiah, and loved to spoil him. Josiah was around sixteen years old at the time, and he relished how Margret took care of him. Over time, we started to notice that he was leaving for school with his bed unmade. Then he would come home, throw his clothes on the floor, and rush out to his next activity. When we confronted him about this, he simply said, "Margret will take care of it." The alarm bells went off.

I would love to say we handled this situation correctly, but to be honest, I'm not sure we did. (Note: Only God is the Perfect Parent, not me or you, and we can take comfort in that.) A mentality was starting to form in Josiah's mind that said, "Someone else will take care of it." And once that mental shift of *entitlement* started, we noticed other areas of his life starting to fall off. Doing his homework wasn't a big deal—besides, his teachers liked him. Why show up early, work hard, and stay late at his soccer practices? The coaches were going to play who they wanted, anyway.

Our son navigated through some dark waters in those high school years. We give thanks to God that He loved our son enough to make him miserable and break this spirit of entitlement in college. He learned the Biblical principle that God, the Perfect Parent, gives responsibility, and when our son embraced that and learned that hard work is a call from God, the doors of blessing started to open for him.

So even if you were like us and failed in this or another area of parenting, don't lose heart. Speak to your child about it, even if they're an adult, and pray, pray, pray to the Perfect Parent to guide your child back to the right path.

Don't be afraid. They can handle it.

Expect great things from your children. Give them responsibilities, and they'll rise to the occasion. And speak life into them. That's what a good parent does.

How to Instill Responsibility in Your Children

Without a goal, you cannot score.
—Johan Cruyff

There are three practical ways to instill responsibility into your children. But before I share them, let me be open with you. We did not instill these concepts into our children until later in our parenting.

Because of our backgrounds, it took my wife and I some time to see how to apply the principles from the Perfect Parent practically into our children's lives. But now that I've seen it in action, I'm excited for our grandchildren, who will fly even higher.

1. Be Accountable

One of the safest, if not *the* safest form of transportation is flying. And one of the keys to the safety of flying is the checklist.

I'll never forget when I was invited to sit in the copilot's seat of a small airplane taking six of us into the jungles of Papua, New Guinea to serve the people there. I was fascinated as I watched the pilot go through his routine. Everything he did was based on checklists. He could not start the plane until the items on a list were checked and verified. He could not pull onto the runway until another list was checked and verified. And so on, until he verified the final list upon our arrival and turned off the engine.

I don't know about you, but I do *not* want to crash and burn in life. I want to fulfill all that God has called me to do. After that flight, I realized that I was thankful for a principle that I had instilled early on into my Christian life: *Set a goal, create action steps to accomplish that goal, and have a checklist to be held accountable for doing the steps.*

Every parent should do this for his or her own life so that they can model this for their children and train them in how to apply it to their lives. Let me give a practical illustration here.

Suppose a young boy named Ross wants to begin skateboarding. He asks his dad for a skateboard. His dad smiles as he tells his son about the plan he follows when he wants something. In fact, his dad informs him that he wants to buy a new car, as the family vehicle needs to be replaced. The father then sits down with Ross and begins to teach him the lessons of **goals, steps**, and **checklists**.

Ross and his father each has a piece of paper and pen in hand. At the top of each paper, they write "Goal." Under it, the father teaches Ross to write out the goal with a specific sentence. He can't just say he wants to buy a skateboard; what kind of skateboard is it, how much is said skateboard, and when does Ross want it? Through this, he teaches Ross the adage that **nothing becomes dynamic until it becomes specific.**

When the details have been nailed down, the tops of their papers read:

> **Ross's Goal:** To buy a SkateXS Beginner Starboard Streetboard for $125 in six months

> **Dad's Goal:** To buy a Certified Used 2019 Ford Escape Titanium for under $20,000 with less than 30,000 miles within one year

Now that the goals have been set, they have some choices to make.

The first possibility is to buy the items right away. That would be easy—one simple step to reach the goal. Unfortunately, Ross only has $60 dollars in his savings jar in his bedroom, and Dad states that he only has $5,000 in savings and another $7,000 or so to work with, given what he could probably get for his current car.

Second, they could ask someone else to buy it for them. For Ross, that would mean asking for it as a present, maybe at Christmas (or asking Grandma to buy it, because Grandma loves to spoil him!). For Dad, he could get a loan to buy it. When you really think about it, this is a subtle way of letting someone else buy a car for him, since he wouldn't really own the car until the loan is paid off. The father explains to his son that asking other people to buy things for you creates a welfare and dependence-on-others mentality, which goes right over the son's head. But his dad continues by explaining that God's plan is for both he and his son to be productive members of society. They are meant to be the ones who *give to* others—not to become *dependent on* others. Therefore, they look at other options.

Third, since they don't have the money to buy what they want now, each of them could come up with steps on how to obtain the money needed to meet their goals. This takes a little brainstorming, speculating, asking questions, and then asking more questions. Ross quickly learns that doing this alongside someone else is far better than trying to do it on his own. He's glad Dad is there.

Through the process, they discover that Ross receives $25 a month for chores done around the house. The first $2.50 goes to his youth group at church, the second $2.50 goes to paying himself (some call this savings), and the rest he is free to use as he wishes. From this, action steps are written down to achieve his goal. Dad does the same. Now, their papers read:

Goal: To buy a SkateXS Beginner Starboard Streetboard for $125 in six months

- ✓ Step 1: Put $35 from savings into a Skateboard Fund, being wise not to deplete all my savings
- ✓ Step 2: Put $15 a month to the Skateboard Fund from my chore money for six months

✓ Step 3: Take 50% of additional money earned from extra chores or seasonal shoveling and put it toward the Skateboard Fund

Goal: To buy a Certified Used 2019 Ford Escape Titanium for under $20,000 with less than 30,000 miles within one year

✓ Step 1: Put $3,000 from savings and combine with $7,000 for current car (when sold) into a Car Fund
✓ Step 2: Set aside $500 a month from my salary for the Car Fund for one year
✓ Step 3: Umpire Youth Baseball games during the summer and put the expected $2,000 ($50 a game at three times a week for fourteen weeks) earned into the Car Fund
✓ Step 4: Work for H&R Block on the side during tax season and put the expected $3,000 into the Car Fund

Ross is excited to see on paper his dream of owning a skateboard becoming a reality. He also loves seeing that he's acting just like his dad. It makes him feel, well, manly! But his dad quickly reminds him that the process is not over. Ross wonders out loud why, and his dad tells him to look up Jeremiah 17:9. "The heart is more deceitful than all else and is desperately sick; who can understand it?"

Ross is confused. "Dad, what does this verse have to do with our plan?"

"It's easy for us to write down goals on paper and even to develop action steps," Dad explains, "but it is also easy to deceive ourselves into thinking we will actually *do it*."

It will be hard for Ross not to spend his chore money when they go to the store and he's allowed to buy his favorite candy. It will be hard for his father not to be going out for lunch, gradually using up his monthly Car Fund money.

Finally, Dad asks Ross, "What makes you think you will actually do it?"

That's where a checklist comes in—to ensure that Ross and his father both *do* what they wrote down.

After more brainstorming, eating lunch together, and sharing some more questions back and forth, a checklist is formed for each:

Goal: To buy a SkateXS Beginner Starboard Streetboard for $125 in six months

- ✓ Step 1: Put $35 from savings into a Skateboard Fund, being wise not to deplete all my savings
  - o Create an envelope marked Skateboard Fund, place the $35 from savings in it, and have Dad and Mom keep it
- ✓ Step 2: Set aside $15 a month to the Skateboard Fund from chore money for six months
  - o Have Dad and Mom take $15 a month from my chore money and put it in the Skateboard Fund envelope before I even have a chance to touch it
- ✓ Step 3: Take 50% of additional money earned from extra chores or seasonal shoveling and put it toward the Skateboard Fund

Goal: To buy a Certified Used 2019 Ford Escape Titanium for under $20,000 with less than 30,000 miles within one year

- ✓ Step 1: Put $3,000 from savings and combine with $7,000 for current car (when sold) into a Car Fund

- o Create a separate savings account with no fees at the bank and put $3,000 from savings into it to earn interest
- ✓ Step 2: Set aside $500 a month from my salary for the Car Fund for one year
  - o Set up with payroll an automatic deduction of $500 to be sent to new savings account
- ✓ Step 3: Umpire Youth Baseball games during the summer and put the expected $2,000 ($50 a game at three times a week for fourteen weeks) earned into the Car Fund
  - o Set up a meeting with the commissioner of the league
  - o Attend necessary refresher course or training
  - o Ensure that at least two games a week are on my schedule
- ✓ Step 4: Work for H&R Block on the side during tax season and put the expected $3,000 into the Car Fund
  - o Confirm position by October 31
  - o Attend refresher courses in November–December
  - o Calculate pay once figures are released to know how many hours must be worked to meet goal
  - o Set a schedule with my wife to ensure that it is agreeable for both of us

While no plan or process is perfect, the above example does give Ross great hope that his dream of owning a skateboard will become a reality. And through this process, Ross's dad is teaching him far greater lessons than just how to get that skateboard. He is training his son to achieve goals across all sorts of areas.

As Ross gets older, a new goals-steps-and-checklists process begins:

Goal: Go to the Air Force Academy

✓ Maintain a minimum 4.00 GPA during high school
- o Study at least two hours a day
- o Sign up for free tutoring in weaker subjects (Trig, Physics)
- o Find a study partner before each major exam to help with my verbal learning style

✓ Join Jr ROTC during junior year of high school
✓ Perform weekly outreach to community to distinguish myself
- o Join Metropolitan Ministries tutoring program
- o Volunteer for Saturday afternoons
- o Keep documented journal as a reference

Goal: Play linebacker for the Air Force Academy

✓ Make the first goal my main priority (getting in is more important than playing football)
✓ Lift weights four times a week and maintain weight of 210
- o Follow coach's workout regimen
- o Eat four meals a day of a high-protein, high-fat diet
- o Make Sunday my cheat day for fun foods

✓ Study films of famous linebackers
- o Three months before practice begins, obtain films and books of Jack Lambert, Lawrence Taylor, and Ray Lewis

o   One month before practice begins, study the films
    and material obtained

2. Start Small and Start Early

Has the temptation already set in?

You know, when you read a book with practical advice, the
temptation often sets in right away. You want to lay the book
aside and start immediately applying the principles. Read a dieting
book, and the next thing you know, your spouse is wondering
why the refrigerator only contains kale and almond milk! It's easy
to become extreme and try to change your parenting overnight.

I beg you: **Apply these principles slowly and methodically**.

One way I tell young parents to apply this principle is to have
their child make their bed every morning. Even very young
children can be taught to pull their sheets and covers up and
straighten their bed. I don't suggest getting a ruler out to make
sure the corners are 45 degrees or bouncing a quarter on the sheets
to test their tautness. But I am strongly suggesting that your child
learn early to take some responsibility for the bed they sleep in.

If your child is old enough, I suggest you sit down together and
watch Retired Navy Admiral William H. McRaven's 2014
University of Texas at Austin Commencement Address. He
brilliantly discusses the lessons learned while training to be a Navy
Seal and their applications to life.[8] Each principle is worthy of a
dinner discussion with your children, but pay particular attention

---

[8] You can watch the full address at:
https://www.youtube.com/watch?v=pxBQLFLei7o accessed 2/21/2020.

to the first point: McRaven learning to make his bed. His point is that even if you have a bad day, you can come home and take some comfort in the fact you have a made bed, something you accomplished that day.

I can certainly relate. When I was in the United States Air Force, I learned to make a bed in boot camp, and at fifty-seven years old, while I may not do it as neatly or tightly as I learned, I still take time every morning to make my bed. Why, as an empty-nester, do I take the time to make my bed? Because I'm a disciplined person. Surely I don't need to do this. But I do. Even when I'm traveling, I make the hotel bed (it's the reason the maids always smile when they see me in the hall!). I do this because I'm still parenting by action, not by words, to my children. I especially want my grandchildren to see that I pay attention to the small things.

It doesn't have to be making the bed. Perhaps you could instill the minor discipline of hygiene. Have your children wash out the sink every morning when they're done showering and brushing their teeth. Or have them arrange their shoes every night. Be creative. The point isn't the activity as much as it is the daily responsibility of doing it.

Start slowly and methodically. Put a little chart on the refrigerator and work with your child to come up with a unique title like "Changing the World" (which will make sense after you watch McRaven's speech). Every day, inspect the bed, open the closet and see how the shoes are arranged, ensure that the dog has been fed—or whatever specific activity you have chosen. Then check it off on the chart. After about six weeks, you probably won't have to inspect too often, as the habit will be forming, and self-discipline will take over.

Let me share two warnings about applying this principle. First, don't turn into a drill instructor. I love the saying you hear today in many churches: *Growth happens best in the context of relationship.* This is true of instilling responsibility into your child. They need a parent, not a Marine Sergeant breathing down their neck, ready to make them get down and give twenty pushups because they didn't complete their chore perfectly. This often causes resentment and rebellion as the child gets older. Always think in terms of relationship first. Instilling these principles in the context of the relationship will help keep you balanced.

A second caution: It is easy to become slack about the little things when your children get to be around sixteen to eighteen years old. I say this out of failure on my part. The pressure of school and sports and musicals and clubs and a host of other things that seem "important" will tend to push aside the little areas of discipline. Help your teenager stay disciplined in the little things, and the big things will come much more naturally.

3. Be Financially Wise

A final area where we can instill responsibility in our children is through finances. There's no rule on how to do this except one word—and it's my favorite word—be *intentional*.

You may pay your children for doing their chores or give them an allowance or have them do extra work to earn spending money, and that's fine. There is no wrong way to do this, but let common sense dictate your actions. Does paying a twelve-year-old $200 to mow the lawn seem right? Probably not. But, on the other hand, expecting them to do it with zero compensation and thereby not allowing your child any chance to earn money will deprive him or her of a chance to learn how to be responsible with money. As more people choose poorly in this regard, and as individual debt climbs, it is the parents' responsibility to teach their children at a young age the principles for being responsible in this area.

When it comes to teaching finances, one would be hard-pressed to find a better mentor than Dave Ramsey. He has helped literally tens of thousands of people with their finances. I recommend the book he wrote with his daughter, Rachel Cruze, *Smart Money Smart Kids*, for a detailed plan to help your children be responsible with their money. But for people like me who love bottom lines, his short article *15 Ways to Teach Kids about Money* is invaluable.[9]

What practical steps can you start taking today? If your child is a preschooler or kindergartner, Ramsey recommends using a clear jar to save instead of a piggy bank. Letting a child see, with their eyes, the money growing when they add to it—and shrinking when they use it to buy something—can have a profound effect. Teach them about savings and celebrate together when it grows.

If your child is in elementary or middle school, some practical things you can do include giving commissions, not allowances. This teaches children that money is earned, not just given to them. You want to raise responsible adults who contribute to society, not suck the life out of it. You can also teach them not to be impulse-buyers by instilling the principle to wait at least twenty-four hours before making any purchase that will require drawing money out of savings. The principle of generosity should also be introduced at this age. Teach your children to tithe. Set aside a percentage of their earned money to give to their church or local

[9] https://www.daveramsey.com/blog/how-to-teach-kids-about-money accessed on 2/21/2020

charity. Let them start to discover for themselves that the healthiest people, spiritually and emotionally, are the ones who believe and practice that it is more blessed to give than to receive.

For teenagers, a key concept to pass on is that of compound interest. Let them see how money grows by investing. Ramsey gives great advice when he says that since teens are on their phones anyway, you might as well download a budgeting app and help them budget the income they earn. And finally, I believe, along with Ramsey, that helping your teenager figure out how to *make* money will be one of the most crucial things you can do. As a result, your teenager will learn entrepreneurship and leadership skills that can never be taught in a classroom. Set aside a special time for you and your child to brainstorm ideas—start a lawn care business, bake cupcakes for special events, or get their first job in the marketplace. The opportunities for teaching your children financial life lessons are endless.

Embrace the Conflict

If, as you reflect on this chapter, your reaction is to think, *This is too much for my child*, then Houston, we have a problem.

Giving your child responsibility is to begin nudging him or her out of the nest so they can soar to new heights. The audacity to **believe in greatness in your child** separates a great parent from an average or below-average one. Help them at an early age to set goals that will push them, and then rejoice wildly when they achieve those goals.

While the skateboard scenario presented in this chapter was a composite of parenting tips I've learned, a parent whom I admire did something that really set a standard in my mind. When his son achieved his own "skateboard" goal, he took him on a three-day mini-tour of famous skateparks in Southern California to celebrate his achievement. What message do you think this sent to his son? Set goals, achieve goals, and life will be better than if you don't.

Lastly, I would encourage you to copy down the following famous quote from Teddy Roosevelt. When speaking with young parents who tell me how difficult parenting is—or that their two-year-old is exhibiting that all-too-common behavior that bears the name "the terrible twos"—I love to tell parents to *embrace the conflict*.

Parenting is hard. It's not for the faint of heart. But we have to embrace the conflict because your child is worth it—oh, so *very* worth it, in the end.

> *It is not the critic who counts; not the man who points out how the strong man stumbles, or where the doer of deeds could have done them better. The credit belongs to the man who is actually in the arena, whose face is marred by dust and sweat and blood; who strives valiantly; who errs, and comes short again and again, because there is no effort without error and shortcoming; but who does actually strive to do the deeds; who knows the great enthusiasms, the great devotions; who spends himself in a worthy cause; who at the best knows in the end the triumph of high achievement, and who at the worst, if he fails, at least fails while daring greatly, so that his place shall never be with*

those cold and timid souls who know neither victory nor defeat.[10]

—Theodore Roosevelt

Dare to enter the arena. Dare to believe and expect great things from your child. And watch them soar.

The Five Principles in Action

Jacob

"When I was a teenager, my parents were called to ministry in the Middle East, which meant moving the family from a small town in Ohio to a bustling city in Egypt. A story came out of this that perfectly exemplifies my dad's philosophy on giving your kids responsibilities.

"When I was sixteen and Joshua was fourteen, we were in the process of moving to our new apartment in Alexandria, and we found ourselves at the airport in Cairo with an electronic piano that needed to get to our new place—a three-hour train ride north of Cairo. We needed to get this piano home, but Dad had business in Cairo. So he hailed a taxi to take me and Joshua to the train

---

[10] These famous lines by Theodore Roosevelt are taken from a speech given on April 23, 1920 at the Sorbonne in Paris titled, "Citizenship in a Republic." You may read the whole speech at http://www.theodore-roosevelt.com/images/research/speeches/maninthearena.pdf

station. We loaded the piano in the trunk of the taxi, and he handed us money to buy tickets for the train and told us, 'Here you go. Get this piano home. It's your responsibility.' That's just how it was with my dad—he and Mom wanted us to improve in our abilities as we matured. At times, that meant trusting us to handle things that felt beyond our capacity.

"I think that being given those responsibilities has taught me to take more ownership of things in my life. It's helped me to be willing to take risks. (And, by the way, the piano did make it home.) I grew up knowing that trying things and failing was okay. I think the flipside, too, is that some responsibilities weren't as high. I'm terrible at cooking! Mom always took care of that!"

Joshua

"There was always an expectation that we were to contribute to our family. When you opened something, you were to close it. When you turned something on, you were to turn it off. And cleaning up after yourself was a given. Dad was big on telling us, 'Your mother is not your maid.'

"Before the move to Egypt, we had household chores like cleaning up after dinner, doing dishes, mowing, cleaning, raking leaves, shoveling snow, etc. After the move to Egypt, the responsibilities often took on different forms. Just before finals my sophomore year of high school, my parents left me behind in Egypt to finish up school. They gave me a plane ticket from Cairo International Airport and an envelope of money. At sixteen, it was up to me to find a friend to stay with, transit on the right day and time to Cairo, and take an international flight by myself. That level of trust and responsibility is unheard of today. My parents were never afraid to tell us, "I need you to take care of this, and I'm not going to tell you how to do it. You figure it out.'"

Bethany

"My parents were good about involving us at home and at church. For instance, when I was just eleven or twelve, they encouraged me to work in the nursery at the church for a while and to take on those responsibilities. And I saw that it wasn't a one-way street; my parents always lived out strong examples of taking responsibility for other people around us.

"At home, there was an expectation that our house was to be neat and tidy, and that responsibility fell on all of us, not just my parents. Dad would say things like, 'Are *you* taking care of *your* house?' But whatever we were doing, I always knew we were in it together as a family. If we were cleaning the house, we were usually doing it together—spending time together, dancing around, and enjoying one another's company."

Josiah

"In this chapter, Dad shared with you a story about me and Margret the domestic worker. What I'd like to add to that story is that those were some really dark years for me personally. There was a lot going on in that season that my parents didn't know about. It was not a fun environment in those days, and sometimes, I felt like a bit of a latchkey kid.

"There had always been high standards for how our home was to be kept, and all teenagers naturally rebel. I knew that having a clean room was one of the most important things to my parents. My actions in being untidy were *intentional* because I was rebelling. But God's grace saw us through that season."

Self-Assessment Questions

1. Before you ever thought of parenting, how was responsibility formed in your life? In what areas did you thrive, and where could there have been improvement?

2. What is your reaction to the **goals, steps,** and **checklist** concept? Is it practical, or can you think of a way to improve it?

3. Small responsibilities like making your bed or washing out the sink were mentioned in this chapter. How are these played out in your view of parenting? Do you think they're necessary?

4. How was financial responsibility taught to you? Do you have a plan to instill it into your children's lives? Why or why not?

Chapter Four:
Principle Three: Set Boundaries

The LORD God commanded the man, saying,
"From any tree of the garden you may eat
freely; but from the tree of the knowledge of
good and evil you shall not eat, for in the day
that you eat from it you will surely die."
Genesis 2:16–17

If I ever had a problem, my parents never had
a problem telling me I had a problem.
—Michael Jordan

When my family lived in Texas, there was a creek in our backyard that our kids would often play near. Normally, the creek was narrow enough that the kids could easily walk across it. But one day, we received heavy rains for twenty-four hours. We had a taste of what Noah must have felt like. Then the rain stopped, and the kids went outside to play. But that harmless little creek that was usually so fun to play in was now a raging blast of white water. I had heard about flash floods but had never seen one with my own eyes. We quickly called our children back inside. The water was too high, too fast, too dangerous.

You see, when a river stays within its banks, it's manageable. It presents little harm. But once a river overflows, destruction comes. And so it is for a child who does not have boundaries set. They grow up to become like a raging river whose banks overflow, and they destroy things in their path. The child becomes an adult and destroys her marriage because she doesn't understand boundaries. She loses her job because she feels too confined in obeying the rules. Her finances spiral out of control because boundaries on spending seem ridiculous to her.

For this reason, the Perfect Parent, God, **sets boundaries**. And He did this for our good!

People have this incorrect concept that God is some sort of Cosmic Killjoy out to squash our happiness. The world thinks the God of the Bible is an angry man in the sky. Ha! Nothing could be further from the truth.

God is fun! God is life. He sent His Son to give us life and to give it abundantly. But our Heavenly Father understands that we need boundaries in order to become all that He wants us to become.

God is a joyous Father who wants His children to be happy and to enjoy life. Look at Adam and Eve. He placed them in paradise with beauty, freedom, and no pain or sorrow—everything a person could want. And in His Sovereign plan, He set a boundary.

> *The LORD God commanded the man, saying,*
> *"from any tree of the garden you may eat freely,*
> *but from the tree of the knowledge of good and*
> *evil, you shall not eat, for in the day you eat*
> *from it you will surely die."*
> **Genesis 2:16–17**

It was not difficult for Adam and Eve to understand this. God didn't come up with some elaborate scheme to test them. His goal was for them to enjoy themselves, but in order to do that, He needed to set a boundary.

Many parents know that they should place some boundaries on their children, but they're not sure how to set them. Thus, they easily fall into traps.

A good phrase to remember is: *God says what He means and means what He says.* God told Adam and Eve to go and enjoy all of the Garden. Yes, He wanted them to have a good time. And part of that included setting up a boundary. He told them not to eat from the tree of the knowledge of good and evil. And for every boundary, there is a consequence. If you eat it, you will surely die.

God set a boundary, and He expected them to keep it. As a good parent, you need to do the same.

Types of Boundaries

You best teach others about healthy boundaries by enforcing yours.
—Bryant McGill

For the modern parent, setting boundaries can be confusing.

For a period of time, I made it a point to simply observe how other parents parented. It was a fantastic exercise, and I learned a lot. From my observations, I noticed three patterns of how parents set boundaries.

These are not laws, just simple observations. However, see if any of these resonate with your own observations on parenting, or maybe even resonate with *your* parenting!

Choking Boundaries

The popular term for parents who exercise these types of boundaries is **helicopter parents.** You know the ones. They hover over their children, making their decisions for them and restricting their ability to learn for themselves. They are a teacher's worst nightmare because they are always questioning the teacher. "Why are you picking on my Archie?" "Why isn't Ava getting more attention?" "How dare you give James a C? It was your lack of instruction that caused him not to achieve more!" If you think these are outrageous examples, they are not. I encourage you to sit down with a teacher and ask them about helicopter parents.

A classic example we are seeing more and more of these days is helicopter parents seeking to protect their kids' health by strictly controlling their nutrition, never letting them eat junk food. Everyone at the birthday party is eating a piece of cake, except poor Mia. She has a bag of carrots that her mom packed and demanded that she eat. No food allergies, mind you; just good nutrition. And what happens when Mia gets old enough to be away from her mother's clutches for a few hours? She binges on sugar like a panda in a bamboo patch! The very thing the mother tried to prevent in her child can easily become a stronghold in the child's life.

Notice how God set His boundary. He told Adam and Eve what they shouldn't do, and then *He let them go free in the Garden.*

God is no helicopter parent, and He does not set choking boundaries. He wasn't there trying to prevent the serpent from talking to Eve. No, He understood that making the decision *for* Adam and Eve was not what a good parent does. He set the boundary and gave them the freedom to obey it or not.

Shifting Boundaries

Shifting boundaries can be defined as arbitrary boundaries that are always changing. In contrast to helicopter parents, I like to call these **jet-ski parents**. Because when you ride a jet ski, you don't just go straight, that's no fun. The fun comes from zigging and zagging all over the place—always changing direction and making tight turns. The difference is, when you parent this way, it's no fun for anyone.

But that's how jet-ski parents set the boundaries for their children. One night, they set the boundary and tell their son he has to eat his vegetables. The next night, the parents are tired, and they quickly shift the boundary because they don't want the hassle. But the night after that, they feel strongly about it again and shift back in the other direction, setting the boundary again that he must eat his vegetables—only to pivot back in the other direction and relent because of the hellacious tantrum the son throws.

This back-and-forth never stops. Just like out on the open water, you may go straight for a little bit, but you get bored, or daring, or enticed, and you start to pivot back and forth again. So the boundaries are always moving. "Take just one bite and that will be enough," changes to, "Tonight, you are going to eat them all." Is it any wonder the child does not immediately obey, waiting to see if the rules will change? Is it any wonder the child throws a tantrum every time, just to test if there might be a pivot of the boundary?

Again, the Perfect Parent does not shift. He's an *ocean-liner* going in a straight direction for the voyage. He's not pivoting back and forth, being fickle in the boundary He set. Even when the serpent came on the scene and tempted Eve, the boundary did not change.

Vague Boundaries

In carrying on with my transportation analogy, let's call these parents **highway parents**, because it's their way or the highway. The problem is, they don't take the time to establish what, exactly, "their way" is. Parents who set vague boundaries may establish rules, but they are never clear on the expectations they have for their children.

Highway parents set boundaries that are antithetical to one of my life mottos: *Nothing becomes dynamic until it becomes specific.* Instead of giving a clear, specific boundary, a highway father will simply say to his daughter, "Clean up your room tonight." The child then trudges off to the bedroom, picks a couple of toys off the floor, and then returns to watching TV. Later, the father looks in the room, goes into a fit of rage, and turns off the TV, bellowing at the child for not doing as he told her. He berates the poor child for not cleaning her room—even though she thought she *did* clean it. And so, the daughter is thrown into a pattern of distrust when given an instruction.

One of the best things a parent can do when setting up a boundary is to have the child repeat the boundary and explain what it means. If you tell your newly licensed teenager to keep to the speed limit, that's too vague. Even *you* don't always stay exactly at 35 mph on the side roads or 65 mph on the highway (if you do, you're watching your speedometer too much and should be paying more attention to the road). Instead, be realistic and concrete at the same time. "Son, I want you to stay at the speed limit. But I know you can't keep perfectly at a certain rate of speed all the time. But if I ever catch you going more than 5 mph over the posted speed limit, I will take the car away from you for two weeks. Do you understand?" That is an example of a clear, not vague boundary.

Unfortunately for Eve, we have it recorded that she distorted her Heavenly Father's boundary. The command was clear: Do not eat from the tree of the knowledge of good and evil. But what God made clear, Eve made a little vague. In responding to the serpent, Eve said that God commanded them to not eat of the tree *nor touch it*. Is this a big deal? Well, to any parent, it would be. No parent wants their command to be distorted. The Perfect Parent's command was clear, yet the child chose to distort it and then disobey it. The rest, as they say, is history.

Boundaries without Clear Consequences

> *God gives you freedom of choice; but He doesn't give you freedom from the consequences of those choices.*
>
> **—Anonymous**

So many times, a child hears the *dos* and *don'ts* in life, but they fail to hear the consequences. Again, God not only states clearly what the boundary is, "but of the tree of the knowledge of good and evil you shall not eat," but he also clearly states the **consequences** of violating the boundary: "for in the day that you eat of it you shall surely die." (Genesis 2:17).

Yikes! That sounds pretty intense. Again, God means what He says and says what He means. And so should you.

Never set a boundary with your child without clearly stating the consequences for violating it. When setting consequences, keep in mind the following two criteria.

1. Make Boundaries Clear and Understandable

Your child should be able to repeat in a sentence what the consequences are for breaking a boundary that you set. They must know that there are boundaries that they should not cross. **The boundary should be specific, and the consequences should be clear.**

I learned this the hard way. I used to tell my teenaged kids, "Don't do something stupid." Anytime they were going out at night, that's what I would tell them. Unfortunately, from a parenting perspective, I learned that the word "stupid" means something very different to a forty-year-old man than it does to a sixteen-year-old boy.

Here are examples of specific boundaries and clear consequences.

"Son, curfew is at 10:00. If you come home at 10:05, you're not driving the car for a month."

"Daughter, I want you to have everything put away in your room by dinner. If you don't, I'm taking your toys away."

Sound harsh? If so, maybe you need to rethink your idea of what **authority** looks like.

Society is not doing a very good job teaching authority. Have you noticed that? Well, we might not be able to do anything about society as a whole, but we can do something about it in our home.

You must instill in your children the concept of authority, which is vital now more than ever. As parents, we cannot and should not rely on schools and society to train our children on how to respect authority. It must be us who instills that in them. A good place to start is to show your kids that you have the authority to set boundaries and to hold to them.

2. Make the Punishment Fit the Crime

Your child forgetting to clean their room before going out to play is obviously not the same as blatantly lying about how the money in your purse disappeared. The former could have been a case of forgetfulness or a simple mistake, but the latter was an act of willful deception.

While there is no clear-cut rule for which punishment fits with which violation of a boundary, I believe a good starting point is to look at the seven things God hates in Proverbs 6:16–19. Make violations of those boundaries more consequential than other violations. Below is a chart as an example. The consequences are random, some applying to small children and some applying to teenagers.

Seven Things God Hates and So Does This Family	Consequence
Pride	Do your chores and siblings' chores for a week
Lying	Wash mouth out with soap
Violence	Stay in room until bedtime, no electronics, write "peace" 100 times

Scheming	Stay in room until bedtime, no electronics, write "love" 100 times
Joining in bad things	No electronics for one week
Not confessing the truth of what happened	Grounded for the weekend, write a two-page essay on the history of perjury and why it matters
Causing conflict	Pay $50 fine paid to the family vacation fund

The Power of No

The oldest, shortest words—"yes" and "no"—
are those which require the most thought.
—Pythagoras

Remember that "No," is a complete sentence. This is a non-negotiable principle for every parent.

You don't need to explain yourself. **Don't give reasons.** Don't feel obligated to provide a basis for your decisions or to justify the boundaries that you set.

In many cases, God did not give reasons for the boundaries He set. Think of the Ten Commandments. They read, "Thou shalt not" or "Thou shalt." Our Perfect Parent doesn't feel the need to explain Himself. And neither should you.

As soon as you start getting into the explanations, you're supplying your children with their reason for an excuse. Your child is sitting there, listening to the reason for your discipline, and gets to thinking, "My argument is actually better than that. I think this is an exception. Maybe I won't do it."

And we *wonder* why our children are confused.

I'm a theologian. I love academia. But there's a new trend originating from these crafty modern theologians. "Well, sure— God did say that. But let's go back and look at the cultural context. Here's why God said not to do that. Our culture is different today, so what was wrong for them is okay for us to do. . . ."

Sounds pretty smart. But wait a minute. God didn't give His reason for why He said that. That's *your* reason or, more accurately, your *explanation of God's reasoning*. It's just someone's way of finding an excuse to justify a decision to not follow His boundaries!

When it comes to boundaries, it is abundantly clear when God says no. Sometimes, that's all He says, and we have to accept that. For some people, that's a hard pill to swallow. Especially if they don't like the command. But that doesn't give us an excuse to not obey God. We need to understand the consequences that come with it.

Why do I tell you this? Because it ultimately will help you be a better parent! Now you understand how your child feels if they don't like the command you have given them. Your child may not like the command "clean your room" any better than you like "love your enemies." But just as you don't have to explain yourself to your child or provide a reason why he should clean his room, so God doesn't explain to you why you should love your enemies.

A command does not need to be explained. And this applies even more so if you trust the person who says it.

The Five Principles in Action

Jacob

"I'll be honest. There were a lot of times when I felt that the boundaries my dad set were overkill. But what helped me was that I always saw the 'why' of it. As I grew older, that helped me realize that I was the type of person who needed a why. I try to remember that and to implement that into my parenting."

Joshua

"When we were young, we lived in a national park. We had a lot of freedom. We would go out and play with neighborhood kids until we heard Mom blow a whistle, which meant it was time for dinner, and we were expected to *be there on time*. I remember being by myself, at eight or nine years old, literally miles and miles from my house and huffing it back home so I wouldn't be late for dinner. I knew there would be consequences if I missed dinnertime. We had a lot of freedom, but there were also clear-cut boundaries and consequences.

"As kids get older, I think you have to reduce boundaries and increase communication. Once they're outside of your boundaries, your kids will inherently be exposed to bad stuff. You can't prevent that, so preparing them through good communication is imperative.

"When we were living in Egypt and I was fourteen years old, I started dating a girl whose father worked at the embassy. One weekend, I wanted to go visit her. Dad said, 'Okay. You know what right is. Choose right. Here's some money. Go ahead.' There was so much opportunity for me to do wrong on that weekend trip, but I didn't. I remember coming back on that train, thinking, 'Wow. My dad trusted me. I didn't sin. I could have, but I didn't.' That was so much more meaningful.

"With my parents, it was always love over law. I had friends with super conservative Christian parents who grew up in far more restrictive environments. Looking back, I see that the kids who had ultra-strict boundaries often didn't feel a lot of love from their parents. Today, most of those guys aren't walking with the LORD. Some aren't even Christians."

Bethany

"My parents' boundaries were always very clear. There was nothing confusing about it, which provided a lot of stability. Having four daughters myself has shown me that things sometimes need to be changed for the sake of sensitivity. My parents would probably say that that was an area where they could have done a little better, but that's the point: Parenting is a learning process for all of us, and every child is unique."

Josiah

"My parents could have kept us in the ideal family environment in Ohio. Instead, they chose to radically follow Jesus, and we moved from a small town to a city of 7 million people on the other side of the world.

"In Egypt, it was the real world. We were no longer sheltered within a safe Christian bubble. As a result, there was a lot of hard stuff that my family went through, but we continued walking with the LORD throughout the hardships. It's a reminder that, for refinement, a bit of heat is sometimes necessary.

"I remember a few times when I went out alone in Egypt. I got caught in my first anti-US protest when I was eleven. We developed enough street smarts to operate in this strange new world thanks to the freedom our parents gave us."

Self-Assessment Questions

1. What kind of boundaries have you set for your children? Are your boundaries consistent and well-defined, or are they choking, shifting, or vague?

2. Do your boundaries have clear consequences? What can you do to improve in this area?

3. Do your children know that "No" is a complete sentence, or do they expect you to explain yourself?

4. Do you love God's instruction? Do you honor His boundaries? Or do you try to find excuses to get out of them?

Chapter Five:

Principle Four: Keep Your Word and Discipline

For those whom the LORD loves, He disciplines,
and He scourges every son whom He receives.

Hebrews 12:6

Discipline yourself and others won't need to.

—John Wooden

When did the idea of **discipline** become a negative for parents?

The world has so skewed the idea of discipline that many parents are afraid to do it. Or, worse, think it is evil to do it. But look at the Perfect Parent.

As we discussed in the previous chapter, He set a boundary: Don't eat from the tree of the knowledge of good and evil. He gave the consequence: The day you eat it, you shall surely die. And what happened when Adam ate from the tree? God kept His word. For Adam died spiritually, which means he no longer dwelt in the presence of God. LORD

> *Therefore the LORD God sent him out from the*
> *garden of Eden, to cultivate the ground from*
> *which he was taken. So He drove the man out;*
> *and at the east of the garden of Eden He*
> *stationed the cherubim and the flaming sword*

which turned every direction to guard the way
to the tree of life.

Genesis 3:23–24

Not only did Adam die spiritually, but God kept His Word, and Adam died *physically* as well.

So all the days that Adam lived were nine
hundred and thirty years; and he died.

Genesis 5:5

You see, God means what He says and says what He means.

Ever wonder how the story would go if a modern-day person was writing the script? You can imagine the twenty-first-century author portraying God as some apologizing father, saying, "Oh Adam, I'm so sorry you ate the fruit! Oh, how terrible. . . . Maybe it's my fault. I must have done something wrong. Let me create another tree, and let's try it again. And please, try not to eat from that tree again. Next time, I will have to punish you!"

No. **God means what He says and says what He means.** There is a consequence for stepping over His boundaries. You have to suffer for it.

"But that's so cruel!" the majority of modern Western society would likely respond. "How could you punish innocent people? Everyone makes mistakes. It wasn't as if Adam and Eve killed anyone!"

Well, it's not cruel. What's cruel is *not* keeping your word and failing to discipline your child.

How many brokenhearted mothers have seen the reality of Proverbs 29:15, "The rod and reproof give wisdom, but a child who gets his own way brings shame to his mother"? I cannot tell you how many times I've sat across from a grieving older parent whose child is wayward. One can feel the pain and shame as they share their story. It reminds me of the truth in the saying, *You're only as happy as your least happy child.*

But it doesn't have to be that way.

I'm Not Going to Tell You Again. . . .

> *If you want your child to accept your values when he reaches his teen years, then you must be worthy of his respect during his younger days.*
> —James Dobson

One time, during my travels, I was seated on an airplane next to a young father who was with his five- or six-year-old son. Whatever the definition of a hellion is, I'm pretty sure this young boy fit the description. He kept kicking the seat in front of him. Jumping up and down on his seat. Yelling that he wanted this or that. The looks people around him gave the father were frightening to behold.

Having studied and taught parenting for many years, I find that my ears always perk up when I hear a parent say, "That's the **last time** I'm going to tell you to stop it." After hearing the father of this little boy on the plane repeat this phrase twice in a matter of minutes, I decided to count. By the end of that short flight, I counted over thirty times hearing that phrase or its siblings (e.g., "I'm not going to tell you again to act right," or, "You're going to get in trouble if you keep doing that").

It was maddening. I wanted to grab the guy and say, "Is **this** your last time?!" Thankfully, God gave me a moment of grace.

Do you think the child ever settled down? Of course not. That is, not until I pulled some candy out of my bag and asked permission from the father to give some to his son. With a look of relief in his eyes, the father consented. I became the hero of the flight. The kid calmed down as he spent his time with his lollipop and other candies. People were literally—and I mean literally—giving me high-fives as I exited the plane!

People can see the damage that comes when a person doesn't keep his or her word. This father did not understand that *you must mean what you say and say what you mean*. When a parent sets a boundary, makes the consequences clear, *and doesn't follow up on it*, well, the results can be devastating.

Here is something important to ponder: **A child doesn't know the difference between a broken promise and a lie**. The father on that plane didn't keep his word. To his child, he was just a liar. It sounds harsh, but it's true.

Think about this:

- You ultimately **lie to your child when you don't follow through with discipline**.
  - I call this *passive* lying. By not keeping your word, you passively lie to your child.
  - The opposite of this is integrity. Telling the truth. That's why Adam had to die, because God cannot lie (Titus 1:2) and He hates lying (Proverbs 12:22). And so should we.

- Because you lied to them, **your child will instinctively know that you cannot be trusted because you don't keep your word.**

  - That is why so many children argue with their parents and don't accept what they say. Because they've witnessed a pattern of passive lying.

- Your child will ultimately **know you didn't love them enough to discipline them.**

  - A parent disciplines their child *because they love them* (Proverbs 13:24).

  - The world has it backward. Movies and television portray the parent who disciplines their child as mean and angry, and show the permissive parent as loving and levelheaded. In reality, it is the exact opposite. If children don't learn consequences through discipline at home, why *shouldn't* they steal from their employer? Cheat on their taxes? With a skewed idea of consequences comes a skewed idea of ethics.

The bottom line in this: If your child sees you as someone who does not tell the truth and does not follow through on your word, you'll never have the respect of that child. One of the greatest things you can do right now for your child is to set the boundaries and keep your word.

You Don't Need to Explain Yourself

I don't want to spend my life explaining myself.
You either get it, or you don't.
　　　　　　　　　　　　—Frank Zappa

It's possible to have too much of a good thing. A rope is a good thing to a drowning man. But throwing him both ends is too much of a good thing. Similarly, if we as parents try to do everything for our children and give them everything, it will be too much. You must give them just enough rope to pull themselves through life, not so much that they drown.

Remember, parent: "No" is a complete sentence. We touched on this issue in the previous chapter, but it bears repeating here. It amazes me how many parents feel the need to explain things to their children.

A typical scenario looks like this: A mother tells little Johnny that he must finish his homework before he's allowed to play his favorite video game. She sets the boundary "Finish your homework" and lays out the consequence, "You won't be able to play your video game until you are finished." Pretty straightforward parenting. But then comes the misdirection that throws many parents off. And it starts with that famous word all two-year-olds know by instinct: "Why?"

Johnny proceeds to ask his mother why he needs to finish his homework. He can do his homework after dinner, but *now* is the best time to play his video game. His mother starts to reason with him. "It's better to get the important things out of the way before you play," she correctly replies. But Johnny doesn't take it lying down. He explains to her that he can process his homework better after eating and getting some food in his stomach and some energy to his brain. Actually, Johnny is pretty proud of himself for that argument, and even his mother is slightly impressed.

Now the mother is on the defensive. She still has time to turn this around, but she chooses the wrong path and begins to *explain* her reasons for setting the boundary and consequence. Johnny, however, is up to the challenge. Like a good lawyer, he has a counterargument for every reason given. Soon the mother is exhausted from arguing and gives in, and Johnny runs off, triumphant in besting his mother in the debate. This scenario not only produces a negative result but also sends a clear message: Mom's boundaries only need to be followed *if they make sense to Johnny.*

Some parents may see nothing wrong with this. They may congratulate themselves for being "reasonable" or even feel proud that they are raising a child who rationally questions authority. But trust me—**this is a precedent you do not want to set with your children.** As long as Johnny can come up with what he feels is *a good reason* for stepping over the boundaries set by his mother, he can now feel entirely justified in disobeying her. This only paves the way for future grief.

The Perfect Parent Disciplines His Children

How do you prevent a little sociopath from becoming a big, full-blown sociopath? Sit on him.

—John Rosemond

Did you notice that God never provided the reason why death was the consequence of Adam and Eve's disobedience?

Why didn't He discipline them in some other way? Why didn't He beat them? Or put them in prison? Why death? And why the tree of the knowledge of good and evil, specifically? Why only that one tree? Weren't there other trees He could have chosen? The questions are endless. . . .

Our Heavenly Father set a great precedent in the Garden by not explaining Himself to His children. He's the Parent. He sets the boundaries, He determines the consequences, and that pretty much settles it.

But that is so foreign-sounding. It seems almost offensive to our "it's all about me" culture. After all, aren't we entitled to some answers?

We feel we have a right to know the reasons for things. Then and *only* then can we determine if we will follow them or not. But God loves us too much to give in to our sentimental feelings. He is the Heavenly Parent, and we are not. Therefore, He has the right. And we as His children have the obligation to obey Him.

But our God is in the heavens; He does whatever He pleases.

Psalm 115:3

As parents, Paula and I found this difficult at first. We tended to want to explain ourselves out of respect for our children. But when we noticed that they always seemed to argue back or try to counter our explanations, we came to realize why God parented the way He did. We learned a valuable lesson. "No" is a complete sentence.

No longer do we feel the need to explain ourselves. We've fallen back on that old country wisdom that says, "I'm the parent, that's why. End of argument."

To be clear, I am not advocating being a fanatic about this. If a teachable moment arises to help your child advance in wisdom, then by all means explain your reasoning. Common sense will tell a parent when their child wants to learn and when they are just challenging the boundary.

Note: Discipline Does Not Equal Abuse

The world has crept into the Church in many ways, and unfortunately, it has ruined a lot of parents.

As soon as you start talking about disciplining your child these days, a major concern arises. What will people think? What will people say? Is Child Protective Services going to come and take my children away? If a child can call CPS and be removed from their home just for a spanking, then we have truly given children the upper hand.

Abuse is obviously wrong in every way. But just because there are evil people who abuse their children, should zero discipline be allowed?

It's common sense that disciplining your child isn't beating them. But many of us are so afraid that it will be seen that way that we don't even discipline them properly. And then we're surprised when our children grow up with no concept of authority.

Discipline is not the same as abuse. If you love your child, you will discipline them, and if you do things God's way, there will never be any risk that your discipline could be misconstrued as abuse. And this is key: Discipline also does not mean punishment.

You don't discipline your child to punish them. Punishment is revenge. Punishment is to put you in your place and make you feel bad; discipline is to bring you back. It's meant to bring you back to your senses. And God disciplines those He loves.

Historic Parenting is Counterculture

> *Children are rarely taught critical thinking anymore, and society has become so antirational that basic reason and evidence are the new counterculture: thought is the new punk.*
>
> **—Stefan Molyneux**

Of all five principles learned from the Perfect Parent, the concept of discipline will surely be the most difficult for people in Western culture to understand.

Eastern culture has, by and large, maintained an understanding of authority, and this is especially true when it comes to parents. Honor toward parents is unquestioned in Eastern culture. No one would fault a parent for physically disciplining a disobedient son or daughter. But in the West, with our antiauthority paradigm, to hear that a parent has physically disciplined—again, *disciplined*, not abused—their child seems absurd. Haven't we progressed beyond such barbaric forms of parenting? Have our verbal and nonphysical forms of punishment not proved superior?

I challenge you, if you live in the West, to **rethink what you know about discipline in your home**. Or, better yet, rethink your view of discipline in light of how you were raised. I am not trying to compare societies and cultures or to suggest that one is better than another. But I am suggesting that Eastern culture has maintained a form of parental discipline that is closer to the way the Perfect Parent disciplined.

So I caution you: Don't let culture obscure the beauty of the Way of the Perfect Parent.

The Five Principles in Action

Jacob

"Dad always instituted teaching components into discipline. There were certainly times when he said 'no' and didn't give a reason, but even when we didn't fully understand, my parents communicated their intentions for raising us under God's word. We knew that discipline wasn't arbitrary.

"I fully admit, I was a pretty strong-willed kid. We butted heads a lot, but Dad wasn't afraid to lay down the law and enforce discipline—and strongly at times. I remember well making the long march to the tree to pick out my switch. I never felt that spankings were done out of anger. You never doubted that it was all done in love.

"I would say I discipline my kids in similar ways, although we've been able to move away from physical discipline as they've gotten older. We never made our kids pick out a switch. Instead, we used a spoon. I mention this because I think it's important to have a single, physical object that represents the consequences."

Joshua

"I remember going to pick out my switch. That was often the worst part—breaking off the branch of the tree to get spanked with it.

"My parents never used their hands. Instead, there was an object of discipline. When I was older, the manner of discipline shifted. I remember not being allowed to drive my car for a while because of missing my curfew. We also had a big five-gallon water jug for the vacation fund and had to pay money into that for saying bad words.

"I agree with my dad that kids don't always need to know the 'why.' They need to understand the concept of obedience. I also think consistency is important: explanation, discipline, and aftermath. 'This is what is going to happen, it was a product of your choices, and we hope you make better choices next time.'"

Bethany

"My dad's favorite saying was, 'My house, my rules.' When you broke those rules, you knew what was going to happen. Even as a child, I understood that boundaries and discipline had love behind them. The message was, 'Okay, Bethany, that was not good, but you are loved.' No matter what you did, you always knew you had a place to come home to. I saw a united front from my parents. They were always on the same page. That being said, knowing your kid (as an individual) is essential. I know I need to use different tactics for all five of my children.

"I think while our family lived in Egypt, Mom and Dad were a little distracted, but they lived out their love for the LORD. They were, and still are, always willing to grow. They're willing to point out where they could have done better. I see other parents who don't have the humble attitude to acknowledge their mistakes in order to grow their relationships with their kids.

"Mom and Dad lived the example. We saw behind the scenes. Their consistency of living for Jesus meant everything. When you see that sort of intentionality growing up, it's powerful."

Josiah

"When I was about seven years old, I was playing with some kids of my parents' friends, and things started to get rough. We were outside on a winter day and they were shoving my face in the snow, and I finally had enough. The night before, we had watched the movie *The Dirty Dozen*, and I had heard a new word, which I promptly used. When my dad found out about my expanded vocabulary, we had an intense confrontation. Then he drove me up to our friends' house, and I had to go talk to their father and apologize for calling his son a word that was inappropriate. That's what discipline looked like sometimes: accountability for your actions.

"The LORD disciplines the one He loves. My parents certainly got some things wrong, but they were consistent. I think of where many of my friends are today—family friends, childhood friends—and I see a lot of anguish and brokenness. There's one friend in particular I'm thinking of whose parents always did a good job sticking to the 'Christian act,' but there was a great deal of compromise in the lives they actually led. You can't afford to compromise. You've got to commit and live it out."

Self-Assessment Questions

1. What comes to mind when you think of disciplining your children?

2. How were you disciplined? How has it shaped your view of disciplining your own children?

3. Have you ever seen a parent trying to explain and reason with their child while disciplining them? Have you ever found yourself doing it? What was positive and/or negative about this experience?

4. Why do you think Western society has such an aversion to historic ways of discipline? Why do you think Eastern society has, for the most part, retained them?

Chapter Six:
Principle Five: Do Everything in Love

The LORD God made garments of skin for Adam and his wife, and clothed them. Then the LORD God said, "Behold, the man has become like one of Us, knowing good and evil; and now, he might stretch out his hand and take also from the tree of life, and eat, and live forever." Therefore the LORD God sent him out from the garden of Eden, to cultivate the ground from which he was taken.

Genesis 3:21–23

God loves each of us as if there were only one of us.

—Augustine of Hippo

Calvin and Hobbes is a cartoon strip by Bill Waterson in which a six-year-old boy, Calvin, exercises his vivid imagination to recreate the world around him. His constant companion is his toy tiger doll, Hobbes, who becomes a full-sized friend when grown-ups aren't around.

In one particular strip, the two of them have fled in panic up a tree to hide because they pushed the family car down the driveway and lost control of it.

"*There* you are," says Calvin's mother. "Come down so I can talk to you."

"No," says Calvin, peeking out from behind the trunk of the tree, his stuffed tiger Hobbes propped in the branch nearby. "You'll kill us. We're running away."

"I'm not going to kill you," says Calvin's mother. "I just want to find out what happened. Are you okay? Was anyone hurt?"

"No one was hurt," said Calvin. "We were pushing the car into the drive and it kept rolling."

"The car didn't hit anything?" Calvin's mother asks.

"It just went across the road and into the ditch," says Calvin. "That's when we took off."

The next panel features Calvin's mother holding her hands out to her son, welcoming him down out the tree. "Well, the tow truck pulled it out," she says, "and there's no damage, so you can come home now."

"First," Calvin says, "let's hear you say you love me."[11]

For Calvin, that word "love" was the proclamation he needed to hear.

So too with Adam and Eve. They knew God would keep His Word. Now that they had transgressed, were they to die instantly and be banished forever? No, actually God did something extraordinary that many people fail to notice.

It wasn't Adam and Eve who physically died straight away; instead, animals had to die to provide skins to cover Adam and Eve's guilt and shame. This is a picture of the blood that would ultimately be shed to cover our shame and guilt. The blood of

---

[11] *Calvin and Hobbes*, Bill Watterson, June 9, 1989.

Jesus Christ was shed because **without the shedding of blood, there is no forgiveness of sin** (Hebrews 9:22). That's how greatly God hates sin. And it's ultimately how much God loved Adam and Eve. He kept His Word. They instantly died spiritually and would eventually die physically.

If you think about it, God could have left his children in this state of sin. Instead, He covered their guilt. He covered their sense of shame. He loved them so much that He sent them out of the Garden so that they would not permanently be in the state of death. And someday, He would cover not only their spiritual shame with the blood of His son Jesus, but He would cover ours as well. Because He loves us. He's a good Father.

Do you want your child to love you, respect you, and follow a good path to live a righteous life? Then ensure, above all else, that **your child knows that you love them**. That you'll do anything to help them and care for them, and that everything you do for them is because of this love.

The Prodigal Son

Repentance means you change your mind so deeply that it changes you.
—Bruce Wilkinson

You're probably already familiar with the parable of the prodigal son, as shared by Jesus in Luke 15. It's the story of a young man who is so determined not to live according to his father's way that he actually has the audacity to ask for his inheritance *before* his father is even dead! For a father in that culture, few things could have been a greater insult from a son than this. Still, he granted his son's request.

True to his father's fears, this young man didn't possess the maturity to handle such a sum of money. Soon he became like so many modern-day lottery winners or professional athletes who sign big contracts. The day comes when the money vanishes, and they go broke.

The prodigal son went broke. Not just broke, we're talking flat-broke—like, homeless guy holding a sign up on the side of the street broke.

Finally, after hitting rock bottom and reaching a place of disgust, the son decides to go home and ask his father for forgiveness.

Now take a moment and put yourself in the father's shoes. If you're reading this book, there's a good chance (very good chance?), that you're a parent. Picture your son or daughter taking half of your retirement account and wasting it in a disgusting lifestyle. You hear rumors that he or she is involved in shooting heroin, participating in orgies—I mean, really deviant behavior. Don't sugar-coat it. Too many times, we sugar-coat the Bible to make it more palatable. Don't do that here. Feel the emotions start to well up as your life grows harder because of your child. Feel the embarrassment when you see your friends and they ask you how your child is. That's how the father of the prodigal son felt.

The prodigal son's father was hurt. He was frustrated, he was embarrassed, and yes, he was probably angry. Very angry. And can you blame him?

Most of us know the end of the story. The father runs out to embrace his son and welcome him home when he finally returns, but I feel we skip a major part of the story.

You see, showing love has nothing to do with emotions. The father of the prodigal son showed love even though, in his emotions, he probably wanted to strangle his son. Always remember: *Love is an action, not an emotion.*

Love Is An Action

Luv is a verb.
                    —DC Talk

The father of the prodigal son may have felt all sorts of wild emotions due to this situation, but the action of love that he showed, the action of words that he spoke, conveyed forgiveness. **He didn't let emotions dictate his actions.**

What about you? Has your son or daughter done something wildly stupid? I mean, one of those things that when you heard it, you literally blurted out, "How could you be so *stupid*?" That was probably your emotions talking, because if you stopped and thought about it, you probably know why they did it. Because I'll bet you can think of something stupid *you* did in your life that caused your parents to think, "How could my child be so stupid?"

We live in a fallen world. Our children are fallen creatures. "There is none who is righteous, no not one," says the Bible (Romans 3:10). And at a moment in time, your child proved that verse true. But think about this: Do you want to break off your relationship with that child forever because of their stupidity?

That's the question the father of the prodigal son had to ask himself. And his answer was that no matter how bad things got, his relationship with his son was more important. He let his *actions* dictate his response to the son coming home, not his *emotions.*

One last thing regarding the story of the prodigal son. . . . Note that the father did not chase after the son when he left.

Think about that. When our movies and stories convey love, it almost always involves the father and mother going after the child, admitting they must have done something wrong, and asking for forgiveness. That's the worldly response. The truth is, that's not necessarily Godly love. This leads me to my next question.

How Would a Modern Parent Treat the Prodigal Son?

Too much love never spoils children. Children become spoiled when we substitute "presents" for "presence."
—Dr. Anthony P. Withham

The Upas tree, which grows in southeast Asia and Indonesia, has many fabulous stories surrounding it. It grows thick, and all vegetation within its shade is killed. It simply overwhelms everything near it. Likewise, many parents will smother and overwhelm their children so that they cannot effectively grow.

What do you think the story of the prodigal son would have been like if the father had behaved differently? What if he had smothered his son like the Upas tree, overwhelming him, disallowing him to make those mistakes and forbidding him from leaving the farm? The son may never have left and made those many mistakes—which many modern parents would see as a victory—but he also never would have learned those important lessons, and he certainly never would have changed his ways. As soon as his father was no longer there, he would have gone out and made all those mistakes. And by then, he may not have had a father awaiting his return.

The father respected the freedom of his son. He let him go. He didn't chase after him. He let him hit rock bottom. I have met so many parents who keep bailing their children out of the pits they get themselves into, only to have to do it all over again the next time.

True love lets the child eat with the pigs until the child comes to their senses *of their own free will* and repents and comes home.

Don't Bail Your Kids Out

Have you been bailing your child out of their messes, under the misguided understanding of what love is? Please forgive me for being blunt, **but that's not love**. You are preventing that child from confronting their own selfish nature, which is necessary for him or her to turn their life around. Let them know, like the prodigal son's father, that they can always come home, but it must be on your terms, within your boundaries.

To clarify, this is very different than Jesus's story of the lost sheep (Luke 15). The shepherd went and looked for it because it was *lost* and was under his care. This story illustrates for parents that if a bad circumstance happens to your child—say they've been in an accident, have a sickness come over them, etc.—you not only should but *must* go to help them. That is love. In contrast, the prodigal son was not lost. He chose to leave. This is very different, and the Holy Spirit and common sense will lead a parent to know the difference.

As children of the Most High God, we can be grateful that we always have a Father waiting with open arms for us to return home.

Show Your Love

When we love something it is of value to us, and when something is of value to us we spend time with it, time enjoying it and time taking care of it.

—M. Scott Peck

When I meet neglectful fathers who claim that, deep down, they love their children, I ask them, "How are you expressing your love?"

This question usually catches them off-guard. They think they love them because *in their mind,* they do. But **love is about the other person.** What the other person perceives makes all the difference.

Parents, do your children know that you love them?

Again, I wasn't the perfect parent. There came a time while we were living overseas when Paula was back in the States preparing for our daughter's wedding. It was just my son and me. He was a teenaged boy getting ready to graduate high school. He was starting to flex his muscles a bit, and he started to not like my boundaries. (And, as a quick disclaimer, I should mention that I asked my son for permission to share this story with you.)

"Son," I told him, "what I've always told you is that you live in my house, and these are my rules. And if you don't abide by them, then what you are saying is that you are now man enough to go and establish your own house. So, you need to leave this house if you refuse to abide by my rules and go establish your own house."

After that, things got real tense, real quick.

Ultimately, one day, my son just up and left. I had no idea where he went.

My wife called me up that night to ask how things were going. You can imagine that phone call.

"Things are . . . uh . . . great here, honey," I said.

"Where is our son?" asked Paula.

"Well, I don't know."

Paula called again the next day to ask if he was home yet. He wasn't.

"Well, when is he coming home?" she asked.

"I don't know if he is," I had to admit.

On about the third day of this, I realized I was not going to get the parent of the year award. But here was my time to live out the story of the prodigal son. What would *I* do? Chase after him? Tell him I was sorry and beg him to come home? No, I needed to follow the example laid out by my Heavenly Father.

I needed to let my son know he could always come home. Let him know I *welcomed* him home. But I couldn't be a modern-day parent. And the difference between the story of the prodigal son versus modern-day parenting can be summed up in one word: *Repentance*. Repentance simply means changing the direction of one's thinking. And **without repentance, a willing change of direction, coming home means nothing**. This was a decision that the prodigal son—and now, *my* son—had to make for himself.

This went on for days, and still my son was nowhere to be found. But I wasn't going to chase after him because he knew the boundaries. He also knew he could always come home.

My son came home a few days later in tears, repentant, and I was there waiting for him. We worked things out, and today, we have a thriving relationship as father and son. He even worked for our ministry for a while before going out and establishing his own work.

As I love to say, God's Word always proves true. It's not always easy—the world may give you an easier route, it's true, but in the end, that way leads to destruction. **God's way leads to life.** Even in parenting.

What Do You Mean By. . . ?

God loves us too much to indulge our every whim.

—Max Lucado

I close this chapter where many would have started: by defining love. I end with this because I want it to be the last word in our Five Principles.

All Five Principles flow out of a correct understanding of love. And without that correct understanding, the Principles can become lifeless laws that will actually rob your children of the very thing you seek to instill in them.

So how do we define true love? It starts with God, who is the Ultimate Reality (Truth). From Him flows the attribute of love to His creation. Therefore, **to understand love, we must seek to**

understand and know God. We cannot look to anything else to get our understanding of love. Not ourselves, not our parents, and certainly not culture or the media or the arts. To put it simply, as the Scripture does: "God is love" (1 John 4:8), and that is where we must look.

True Love Applied

I love my children. But when I found out that one of them had stolen something and then lied about it to cover up their theft, I became angry. I mean good and angry. And I disciplined them because of my anger.

I write those words fully aware that when people read them, they may immediately misinterpret my message and think that I was being *unloving* to my child because I disciplined out of anger. But where does this notion come from that anger and love are incompatible? Not from God. Scripture is crystal clear that God, who is perfect, gets angry. His anger burns against unrighteousness and injustice (just read Numbers 11–12 for a few examples).

Scripture also tells us that we can be angry and not sin (Ephesians 4:26). So why would I think it is wrong to be angry about two unrighteous acts, stealing and lying? Why would I *not* let that anger drive me to discipline my child so they learn the necessary lesson that stealing and lying are evil and that we must not commit such acts?

So again, why would I place such emphasis on correctly defining and understanding true love in a parenting book? Because for most of us, love as defined by the world has trumped love as defined by God. Because if you seek to put into practice the Five Principles of this book and do it out of your own understanding of love—or the world's understanding—then you and your children are bound to fail. Oh, you may gain some temporary benefits or get short-term goals accomplished, but **you will not have the ultimate blessing because you've replaced God's love with something else.** That is called idolatry. And God's blessing is never with those who have idols in their hearts.

Here is a simple way of seeing how True Love versus Worldly Love can affect the Five Principles:

Create a Good Environment

- *True Love* creates a place of aesthetic beauty with a spiritual reality of no sin.
- *Worldly Love* creates a place of material grandeur with little to no emphasis on spiritual matters.

Give Responsibility

- *True Love* provides a balance of freedom to develop creativity; pressure to promote action and growth; and goals to prevent being overwhelmed.
- *Worldly Love* provides no instructions or gives instructions that are so detailed that it quenches growth and becomes a matter of senseless chores.

Set Boundaries

- *True Love* desires to protect and also to determine a child's wisdom and loyalty.
- *Worldly Love* asks, "Why do we need boundaries?"

Keep Your Word and Discipline

- *True Love* inflicts only enough pain, physical and emotional, to deter and teach the lesson that there is a better way.
- *Worldly Love* always goes to the extreme—either no discipline or cruelty and abuse.

Do Everything in Love

- *True Love* is patient, kind, not jealous or arrogant, but rejoices in righteousness and truth.
- *Worldly Love* makes it all about the individual's own happiness.

In a life-defining moment in the Old Testament, Joshua asked the Israelites to implicitly decide whom they would choose to serve, the LORD God who had led them into the Promised Land, or the gods of this world. Here, I pose the same question to you. Will you choose today who will define love for you and determine the way you parent? **Will you follow the LORD God of the Bible, our Father who is in heaven, or yourself and the world?**

Believe it or not, every single decision in your parenting will flow from how you answer this question.

The Five Principles in Action

Jacob

"Right off the bat, when I think about love, I think about how good my mom was at affirming us. She would always pull us aside, hug us, look us in our eyes, and tell us that she and Dad were proud of us. She was intentional about really speaking love and being purposeful about saying 'I love you.'

"Even when we experienced conflict with one another, things were sustainable because we all shared a common, trained commitment to God as the center of our home. As a result, we were able to endure a lot of the sorts of challenges and heartaches that all families go through, without experiencing the sort of 'relationship drift' I've noticed in other families.

"I've certainly seen people who have managed to grow in Christ without that sort of intentionality, but they are the exceptions. There's truly something unique about the environment we grew up in."

Joshua

"My dad has said this my whole life: 'Be intentional.' My parents were good at that. Coming up with a coming-of-age ceremony, going out one-on-one and being discipled. We even had a father-son fishing trip to Canada. My wife and I implement the same thing with our children. We make time individually with each kid, including "date nights" or "daddy-daughter" nights, ensuring that they're all getting one-on-one time. That kind of investment in them is important.

"The thing that many people overlook is the coaching aspect of parenting. I've seen again and again that the only way to grow a relationship and establish trust is through time.

"In my house, we try to celebrate failure. We know that our kids are going to make mistakes, so we want to sit them down and talk them through it. Proverbs 20:5 says that a person's ways are like deep waters, but a wise person knows how to draw them out.

Bethany

"Even as a child, I understood that love was deep in the seams of everything in our family. The practical application when it comes to parenting girls is to show that emotions are safe to have. Get it out here. Sometimes the world won't understand it, but the home is a safe place to get it out.

"Personally for me, my expression of love was a little different than what my parents knew how to give at the time, but I never felt a lack of love. But even though my needs were different than those of my brothers, I understood my parents' intentions behind everything.

"I truly love being with my family. I feel like that is something that my parents passed down to me, to just spend time together and share love."

Josiah

"My dad is a man who means what he says, and he would sometimes use the phrase, 'I'm your father, I'm not your friend.' He wanted to be our parent because that was his God-given job, which I think is good in a lot of ways. The downside for me, though, is that there were times when I wish my dad *had* been a little bit more of my friend. We still discuss this issue from time to time, and it's a point we've just had to agree to disagree on. That said, it's important to remember that my father grew up in a super dysfunctional home. So did my mother. My parents did not have any examples. They were learning it all first-generation.

"My siblings and I were kind of the 'weird kids' when it came to how we related to adults. We were taught to introduce ourselves to people, shake their hands, and look them in the eyes. From the vantage point of mature adulthood, I now look back and find myself exceedingly grateful that my parents taught me the way they did. We didn't always gel with worldly culture, but we learned the greater principles.

"Everything Dad has shared with you, he's learned from the Lord over time. It's all come from a place of grace."

Self-Assessment Questions

1. In what ways do you show love to your children?

2. Do your children *know* that you love them? How do you know this?

3. Brainstorm at least five new ways that you could show love to your children.

4. Have you ever thought about the way you define love? What are your thoughts on the last section of this chapter regarding how we define love?

Conclusion

Every good thing given and every perfect gift is from above, coming down from the Father of lights, with whom there is no variation or shifting shadow.

James 1:17

Finally we shall place the Sun himself at the center of the Universe.

—Nicolaus Copernicus

There are many great parenting books out there, but when it comes to the day-to-day aspects of parenting, frankly, I can't remember what any of them said.

Perhaps you picked this one up as an excited parent-to-be or a brand spankin' new parent (if so, be encouraged—just by reading this, you are off to a great start! It shows your desire to learn and grow). Perhaps you are a mentor who is desiring to encourage and help others learn to parent well. Or perhaps you are a grandparent who desires to pass down a legacy (as my wife and I do) but haven't quite figured out how to express this. No matter which of these scenarios applies to you, I want to cheer you on. And I also want to remind you of one simple truism:

Less is more.

During the process of writing the book in your hands, I felt pressure from many to expand on it—add chapters to it, make it a full-size book with lots of illustrations. But I resisted. Because in the end, it won't help to tell you a lot if you remember very little.

That is why I've kept it simple: Five Principles that God, as a Perfect Parent, displayed that you can practice, too.

Create a Good Environment

Give Responsibility

Set Boundaries

Keep Your Word and Discipline

Do Everything in Love

It's not complicated. In fact, with a little effort, you can memorize these in just a few moments.

Not only is it simple to memorize these principles, but—yes, I'm going to say it—**they really aren't that difficult to follow.**

But wait.... Isn't parenting supposed to be super complicated? It *must* be difficult! Isn't that why there are whole sections on parenting in bookstores? Isn't this why you can get a PhD in child psychology or early childhood development; because it is so complicated that it takes years of advanced study just to understand it? How could five easy-to-learn and easy-to-apply principles be all it takes to produce a child who will follow the course you have set them on?

The truth is, it really is that easy. That's why your great-grandma would never have understood what these modern parenting experts were talking about. She had common sense. I love how author John Rosemond puts it:

> *Before the 1960s, when parents had problems with their children, they did not seek advice from people with capital letters after their names. Rather, they sought the counsel of elders in their extended families, churches, and*

communities. "Grandma"—the generic term I use to refer to the elders in question—was the universally recognized child-rearing expert. Grandma gave childrearing advice based on the life she had led. . . . After the 1960s, parents were no longer going to Grandma for child-rearing advice. Instead, they were seeking counsel from people in the mental health profession—people who dispensed advice based not on lives they had led, but rather on books they had read.[12]

My generation learned from our grandparents, but we failed to pass it on. And we can see the effect this has had in the West with the breakdown of the family. I'm convinced that Grandma would have looked at these five principles, nodded her head, and said, "Well, yes, that's just common sense!" And it is. But not only is it common sense, it's *Biblical.* What I stated earlier in this book bears repeating: **The Bible always proves true.**

I continue to hear parents claim that the Bible has little to say about parenting. But, my friend, it does!

My wife loves to say, "The principles don't change, although sometimes the particulars do." And although parenting *particulars* come and go, our God and His *principles* never change. The dreams that parents had for their children in the first century are the same as we have today in the twenty-first century. They, like you, wanted a blessed life for their children. And God's Word

---

[12] Rosemond, *Parenting by the Book,* 18–19.

and common sense will provide the best chance your child has to reach that blessed life. Guaranteed.

Therefore, my goal in writing this short and simple book has been to point you to the principles that have proven timeless and to present them as they are revealed and modeled by the very Creator Himself, as a loving Father to His children.

Our Father wants the very best for His children. And so do you. But, as none of us are perfect parents, your charge, should you choose to embrace these principles as your own, is to emulate the One who *is*. For our God *is the Perfect Parent*.

May He find us faithful.

Appendix:
Verses that Support the Five Principles

Parents Are Responsible for Disciplining Their Children

Deut 8:5

Ps 94:12

Prov 3:12

Prov 12:1

Prov 13:24

Prov 15:32

Prov 19:18

Prov 22:6, 15

Prov 23:13–15

Prov 29:15, 17

Eph 6:3–4

Heb 12:5–11

1 Tim 3:4

Rev 3:9

Parents Are Responsible for Teaching and Passing on Faith to the Next Generation

Gen 18:19

Gen 48:15

Ex 10:2

Josh 4:20–24

1 Chron 29:19

2 Chron 34:1–3

Deut 4:9

Deut 6:6–9

Deut 11:19

Ps 78:4

Prov 10:1

Prov 22:6

Isa 38:19

Joel 1:3

Eph 6:4

Tit 2:7

2 Tim 1:5

2 Tim 3:15

Children Are Called to Obey and Honor Their Parents

Ex 20:12

Lev 19:3

Deut 5:16

Prov 1:8–9

Prov 3:11–12

Prov 6:20

Prov 13:1

Prov 15:5

Prov 20:20

Prov 23:22

Eph 6:1–3

Col 3:20–21

Parents Are Not to Provoke Their Children

Eph 6:4

Col 3:21

1 Pet 5:3

Children Are a Gift from God

Gen 1:28

Gen 4:1, 25

Gen 33:5

Gen 41:50–52

Ps 113:9

Ps 127:3-5

Prov 17:6

Jam 1:17

3 John 1:4

God Closes and Opens the Womb

Gen 12:1–3

Gen 15:4–6

Gen 17:15–21

Gen 18:9–15

Gen 20:17–18

Gen 21:1–7

Gen 25:21

Gen 29:31

Gen 30:2, 17, 22–24

Isa 66:9-19

2 Sam 12:16

Parents Are Instructed to Provide Financially for Their Children

Gen 31:14–16

Gen 48:1–49:27

2 Cor 12:14

1 Tim 5:8

Parents Are Called to Protect Their Children

Gen 19:8

Gen 34:5

Gen 30

Gen 33:1–3

Parents Reflect God's Love in Their Love

Ps 103:13

Prov 3:12

Isa 66:13

Luke 11:11

Heb 12:5–11

1 Pet 5:3

God Loves Children

Matt 18:1–6

Matt 18:10

Mark 9:37

Mark 10:13–16

Luke 18:15–17

Parents Should Take an Active Interest in Their Children's Marriage

Gen 24:1–28

Titus 2:3-5

Parents Should Not Idolize Their Children

Gen 22:1–19

1 Sam 1:28

Matt 10:37

Luke 14:26

Children Bring Heartbreak with Sinful Decisions and Joy with Godly Ones

Gen 4:8

Gen 37:31–35

Gen 45:25–28

Gen 46:29–30

Deut 21:18–21

Prov 10:1

Prov 29:15, 17

Parents Should Entrust Their Children to God

1 Sam 1:28

Isa 54:13

Notes